THE
LESBIAN
COMMUNITY

THE
LESBIAN
COMMUNITY
DEBORAH GOLEMAN WOLF

UNIVERSITY OF CALIFORNIA PRESS
BERKELEY•LOS ANGELES•LONDON

University of California Press
Berkeley and Los Angeles, California

University of California Press, Ltd.
London, England

Copyright © 1979 by
The Regents of the University of California

ISBN 0-520-03657-3
Library of Congress Catalog Card Number: 77-93478
Printed in the United States of America

1 2 3 4 5 6 7 8 9

This book is dedicated with affection
to the women in the community

A woman without a man is like a fish without a bicycle
(Graffito in the women's lavatory, Student Union,
University of California, Berkeley, 1975,
attributed to Flo Kennedy)

CONTENTS

LIST OF
ILLUSTRATIONS

ACKNOWLEDGMENTS

This book would not have been possible without the help of a large number of people. Most immediate, of course, are the members of the community who cooperated with me and, by doing so, made the project possible. There are many community members who deserve special thanks; to acknowledge them by name, however, could lead to repercussions for them, which I should like to avoid. It is a sad comment about the nature of our present society that this is true and that a study which documents a community that others might want to emulate cannot acknowledge by name some of the key figures who made that community possible. They know who they are and that I am grateful to them. Special thanks are due to Sally Gearhart, Phyllis Lyon, Del Martin, and Patricia Norman, who acted as consultants, though of course I am responsible for my depiction of the community and for my conclusions.

This book first appeared in the form of a Ph.D. dissertation for the Anthropology Department at the University of California at Berkeley, and for help, advice, and moral support at that stage I should like to thank Drs. Gerald Berreman, David Matza, William Shack, May N. Diaz, and especially Alan Dundes, who got me started in the first place. Part of my financial support during the period of fieldwork was subsidized by a Special Career Fellowship from the Ford Foundation.

At a more personal level, I wish to acknowledge the help and unusual degree of support of my family, Leonard, Aaron, and Naomi Wolf, who lived fairly cheerfully with this work for much

Acknowledgments

longer than they thought they had signed on for. In a more indirect but equally important way, my parents, Fay and Irving Goleman, were very influential.

A note of thanks is due to those who helped to make this book a reality. Joan Mello kindly typed the original manuscript, and Laura Wilensky typed the final version. Laura did more than type; her perceptive comments helped me rethink aspects of the work. I am grateful to Virginia Morgan, Cathy Cade, and Laura Wilensky, who contributed most of the photographs. All three are excellent photographers, whose involvement and contacts added an important dimension to the work.

Finally, I am grateful to Grant Barnes and Sheila Levine of the University of California Press for their encouragement, faith, and tactful suggestions.

1. INTRODUCTION

It was a jubilant historical moment for the confirmed lesbian. The militant gays had moved very fast from the conservative 60s homophile organizations seeking civil libertarian reform and other appeals for integration into society as an "oppressed minority group." The militant Gay now conceived that Gay Liberation was the axis for revolutionary change. This was a momentous series of steps from self-hatred in guilt and secrecy to apologetic pleas for greater acceptance and legal sanctions to affirmation of identity to agressive redefinition in the context of revolution.

Jill Johnston, *Lesbian Nation* (1973), p. 149

The phenomenon of the liberated lesbian has not been adequately described, yet the effects of the women's, gay, and lesbian-feminist movements of the 1960s have irrevocably altered the social role of lesbian and have significantly changed possibilities inherent in that role. From the older pattern of isolation and fear of disclosure, thousands of women across the country have proudly affirmed their lesbianism to be at least as valid as heterosexuality. Proud affirmation of lesbianism was only the first step. In many cities and even in small towns across America, lesbians have chosen to band together to build their own self-sustaining communities, in which social relations based on empathy, egalitarianism, and sharing could take root and

1

1. Lesbian-feminists marching in a Gay Pride Day Celebration, San Francisco, 1975. (copyright: Arts/Unlimited. Crawford Barton)

flourish. Yet most people are unaware of the existence of these communities or of the new, affirming lesbianism.

This book describes the texture of life in a contemporary lesbian community. It examines the lives of single women, women in partnerships, women developing new kinds of relationships, and—an even more significant group, one about which too little is known—lesbian mothers and their children. It focuses on actual behavior, attitudes, mythology, and future goals of a group of women who feel they are forging a new direction in personal and communal life. Through this focus on realities, a radically different picture of the lesbian world emerges, one that may serve as a model for small, self-sustaining urban communities of the future, whatever the affectional preference of their members.

Fieldwork Experience

The research method used in this study was participant observation over a two-year period supplemented by taped interviews, traditionally used by anthropologists in nonliterate societies and transferred with success to studies of societies more similar to that of the investigator (Whyte, 1943, is an early

2

example). I began this study in 1972, approximately five years after the women's liberation movement had surfaced nationally, three years after gay liberation had emerged so dramatically during the Stonewall riots in New York City, a period in which "consciousness-raising" small groups (see p. 67) had been part of the experience of many feminists locally, whether identified as lesbian or not. It was also a time in which the issue of separatism was at its most controversial. Exponents of this view felt that lesbians needed to separate themselves not only from men but also from women who cohabited with men. By doing so, they felt that they would be able to develop strength and direction most effectively by themselves and then, perhaps later, could join in coalitions with heterosexual women or with gay men for particular goals.

The issue of separatism is a legitimate one. especially for a minority group trying to develop a program of action based on a positive sense of identity. However, for a heterosexual researcher it presented problems, which I finally resolved by assuming that if research is ever done on a group of women strongly committed to lesbian separatism, it will be conducted by a member of the group itself.

Every anthropological observer has to decide whether to include controversial data to make the ethnographic description more comprehensive or to take into consideration the wishes and needs of those observed and delete it, especially in a community as vulnerable as this one. My first priority has been to protect the participants; therefore, I have checked everything I have written with members of the community who have been actively involved in it for many years, and whom I trust to have a highly developed sense of nuance about what material might be harmful and to correct any erroneous assumptions I might have made about what I was describing. In fact, there were very few modifications and none which significantly altered the body of work. I consulted with knowledgeable women about events I might not be welcome to attend, and relied on reports of these events if it was felt that such data would not be harmful to the community.

There is some stress, contradiction, and personality clash in all groups. This community is no exception; in fact, since its members take feelings very seriously, a lot of energy is expended in working through personality "hangups" such as jealousy and competition. Some community members attribute these and other negative characteristics to social processes of the culture as a whole, which they perceive as repressive and overly competitive. In presenting a description of the community, I did not overlook this lack of congruence between ideal and actual behavior; yet I did not unduly emphasize this kind of conflict, because it seemed that the more interesting problem was how priorities were defined and what action was taken to put them into effect.

Several factors led to the choice of the lesbian-feminist community as the subject for this study. One of them was the publication in 1972 of *Lesbian/Woman* by Del Martin and Phyllis Lyon. This book was among the first to describe contemporary lesbian life written by admitted lesbians who had worked actively and courageously to change the social conditions of the group to which they belonged. The two women had long urged nonjudgmental research on various aspects of homosexuality by outside "experts." However, they and other lesbians had begun to realize that their own expertise on lesbian life was at least as valid as that of heterosexuals who have more academic qualifications. Also, many academically trained lesbian researchers felt that they could not conduct studies of lesbians, because they might be accused of special pleading, or that to make such a study would expose them as lesbians and thus endanger their careers. Happily, within the last few years, lesbian researchers in a variety of fields have begun to ignore these strictures and have initiated studies of their own group.

In 1972, however, concerned lesbians still felt that if it was too dangerous for a lesbian to conduct this research, the alternative would be a heterosexual feminist researcher. Some community members believed that local lesbians might participate in such a study for two reasons: a woman might be more sensitive to the aspects of lesbian life and of a female-dominated subculture than a man, whose socialization might predispose him to make unwarranted assumptions about lesbians; and because of a commitment to feminism, lesbians might cooperate with a woman in a field traditionally dominated by men.

A further consideration developed from work initiated in a seminar on women conducted by Dr. May N. Diaz at the University of California in Berkeley in 1972. My seminar project entailed looking for sources of strength in women in contemporary urban America. Since I wanted to control as many variables as possible, I chose a group of women who did not derive any aspect of their identity from men—a group of lesbian-feminists. I believed that these women presented themselves in a more self-confident manner than would be typical of a comparable group of heterosexual female graduate students. I was also intrigued by the discrepancy between stereotyped images of lesbians—as "butches" or "femmes," as bar habitués, or more luridly, as primarily sexual creatures trying to convert other women—and the actual appearance, behavior, and self-image of the women concerned. Some of these women had "come out" (identified themselves as lesbians) before the liberation movements of the 1960s, but most of the women that I met at first were "new gay" in that they had come to terms with their lesbianism within the context of an articulated social movement and an already existing community. As I became more involved with fieldwork, it was evident that the phenomenon of post-liberation lesbianism introduced significantly new ideology, self-image, patterns of relationships, and social organization; also, it broadened the expectations about the nature of the social role of lesbian. I decided to expand my seminar project into a full-scale research project.

My first formal contact with the community came when I attended a three-day symposium on homosexuality presented by the Council on Religion and the Homosexual at Glide Memorial Church in San Francisco in the fall of 1972. The first day and a half of the symposium was devoted to the subject of male homosexuality. When the lesbians held their sessions, the presentation differed greatly from that of the male homosexuals. For one thing, they never spoke to the audience from a platform; rather, on the assumption that the "experts" and the audience were equal participants, they arranged the chairs in concentric circles. Compared with the men, they seemed less concerned with whether the authorities of the religions in which they had been raised approved of them and their lifestyle. They had apparently found alternatives to the organized religions that had rejected them. They also seemed less concerned than many male homosexuals with pursuing the goal of freedom to have

uncommitted sexual experiences; rather, they were more interested in enhancing the quality of relationships with both
friends and lovers.

At the end of the symposium, many heterosexual participants
stressed how little was the difference they felt between themselves and the gay men and lesbians who had been present.
Some of the younger and more politically active lesbians, however, said that they didn't give a damn about heterosexual approval, it had become irrelevant to them. The implication was
that while heterosexuals might be well-meaning, it was they—
who were judgmental about homosexuals—who where the
"sick" ones. Liberated homosexuals did not need their approval.

As the meeting ended, a member of the local chapter of the
Daughters of Bilitis, a primarily lesbian organization, announced that the group was looking for new members. I asked if
heterosexual women could join and was told that all women
were welcome. The local chapter was then flourishing. Most of
the active members were in their twenties, had participated to
some extent in women's and gay liberation, and were dedicated
to helping other women adjust to their social identity as lesbians.
Although technically the organization was open to all *women*,
the majority were lesbians.

I began to attend the meetings regularly and through them
became acquainted with some of the women I later interviewed.
However, because of my attendance at these meetings, it was
assumed by some of the other members that I too was a lesbian.
After discussion, the officers of the organization and I agreed
that it would be inappropriate to announce at every weekly
session that I was a heterosexual anthropologist. It was felt that
to do so would cause unnecessary controversy and might in-
timidate women attending for the first time. Besides, as the
president of the organization explained to me, women often
come to the organization saying at first that they are "doing
research." They usually end up coming out as lesbians themselves.

The officers all knew about my project and they often made
useful suggestions. In return I volunteered to do various jobs to
help out in the office. In time, I became the "token straight" in

the organization and was on a comfortable social basis with many of the regular members, with whom I spent a great deal of time outside the organization. During this process, I received a thorough grounding in many aspects of lesbian social life.

At the same time I became aware not only that there was a large population of lesbians who had parallel social networks centered in women's bars, but that there was also an emerging community of liberated women who were developing their own projects and organizations, bypassing the Daughters of Bilitis, which traditionally had been the entry into the lesbian community. Some of these women were trained professionals who were offering their services as feminist therapists or health-care specialists; others were teaching or taking courses on aspects of feminism or lesbian life; still others were working-class women who were banding together to teach each other skills and to offer these skills to the lesbian community at large. As I became acquainted with some of these women, the focus of the research shifted from general participant observation to interviews with specific women.

As an aid in analyzing the phenomenon I was documenting, I used material written by liberated lesbians as well as ideological literature from the feminist and lesbian-feminist movements. These data came from handouts, journals, the underground press, accounts of personal experience, songs, poetry, movies, and other material created by members of the subculture to express their feelings and to describe their experiences.

A shift in direction occurred when I went to a major lesbian conference in Los Angeles in 1973. The conference was attended by an estimated fifteen hundred lesbians; it was said to be the first time "since Sappho" that such a large number of lesbians openly congregated. At least two concepts emerged from the conference that influenced the development of lesbian-feminism on the West Coast. One was the realization that lesbianism itself was no longer enough to serve as a bond between women. As a positive self-image developed among lesbians, women tended to gravitate toward others who shared a political view or a particular talent, or who had something other than their lesbian identity in common. Because of this development, which led to the emergence of different factions at the confer-

2. *Two lesbian poets at a Women's Spring Festival. (Cathy Cade)*

ence, subsequent gatherings were more sharply focused: a very successful three-day conference on women's music was held later, for example.

The issue of class bias also surfaced at the conference. Combating racism, sexism, and heterosexism, as lesbian-feminists had been doing, was no longer sufficient. Class distinction had emerged as one of the crucial factors in dividing women from each other, and women were becoming increasingly aware of how class bias operated to serve the system. Several problem-solving groups intent on overcoming class bias had originated from a workshop at the conference and continued to meet in San Francisco as well as in other cities.

I spent the summer with lesbians in a variety of situations and conducted further interviews based on my sense of the community, which had developed during the preceding period of research. In the fall of 1973, I attended a class on lesbianism that was team-taught by four lesbian-feminists at San Francisco State University. In the class many issues were raised, and in the discussions that followed, some of the implications of community life became clearer to me. I also became aware of how much the various programs of women's studies served to help lesbians meet each other and how such a comfortable, accepting atmosphere drew other lesbians into it, so that from this context women found each other and developed nuclei of social networks, which functioned as an entry into the community for a larger, more political group, much as the Daughters of Bilitis had done earlier.

At the time I was privileged to live in a commune of activist lesbian women, sharing the expenses and upkeep of the house. My husband had taken our children to Jerusalem to settle for the year, while I stayed behind to finish the project; however, an historic event changed these plans. The October 1973 war broke out in Israel, and I immediately abandoned my fieldwork to join my family. Because of this, a change in attitude toward me and my research took place among some of the women who had previously defined me solely as a privileged researcher. Instead, I had become to some of them a mother whose family was in trouble, and although some women still disapproved of the fact that I was studying their community, they became more sympathetic to me personally.

Although the year away from the community made it initially difficult for me to pick up some of the threads, it ultimately helped the study by emphasizing the element of time. It had been a period of national recession in America, and this affected some of the projects in the community. New patterns had developed. Replacing the first flush of enthusiasm in building a lesbian culture was a note of realism and of the need to attend to the problems of survival. What eventually emerged was the vitality of the community and its instinct for survival. Though the process of developing a new social self, new kinds of personal relationships, and a community based on these was slower and more frustrating than had been originally supposed, techniques were gradually being developed to overcome obstacles

9

and to continue the process, while adhering to the original ideological vision of the future. The people concerned had become more street wise.

Since then, both gains and losses have occurred for gay rights in general, and these have affected local community members. After several years, during which gays of both sexes were developing a stronger sense of their rights and were strengthening their own communities, a major setback took place in 1977 with the overwhelming defeat of the Dade County, Florida, ordinance protecting gay rights. This event had national coverage and was seen as a victory for anti-homosexual forces. Many gays felt that this was only the beginning of a strong conservative backlash against them. Some, who had openly participated in community life, felt that more caution was indicated, while others banded together to work harder politically to protect gay rights.

Only a few months later, in November 1977, in San Francisco, the first openly gay candidate was elected to the office of Supervisor, representing a part of the city that, while it included a large number of gay men and women, had an overwhelming heterosexual majority, many of them in family units.

Another important gain for lesbian rights nationally took place when a resolution to support lesbian rights passed by an 8 to 1 margin at the historic National Women's Conference in Houston in 1977.

The overall effects of recent political events on many community members are a stronger sense of the need for bonding; more political sophistication to protect what gains have been made, while remaining alert to indications of anti-homosexual oppression; and a greater willingness to act in coalition with other groups.

A final note on methodology is in order. In all cases the complete anonymity of the women involved has been protected, with the exception of women who are publicly identified as lesbians or are well-known lesbian or heterosexual feminists. I had face-to-face contact with perhaps eight hundred lesbians in the course of the field experience. I worked closely with about thirty women; with three of these I systematically checked my perceptions about the work. I conducted taped interviews with twenty-five women who ranged in age from seventeen to fifty-five. Of these, about two-thirds were middle class in origin, one-third working class. It is likely that a large proportion of the community was unavailable to me, and of these, many were working-class. However, the informants felt that they were speaking for these women at least some of the time.

The informants had a wide range of interests, backgrounds, and positions in the community. The women who were interviewed included a maker of feminist films, a carpenter, women on welfare, several lesbian mothers, a bar owner, a professor, a garage mechanic, a factory worker, and a physician. I had the opportunity to interview many of them again after a year. The cooperation I received from the women who allowed themselves to be interviewed made this work possible.

Tapes ranged from three to twelve hours in length and were mostly structured by the person being interviewed. The only questions I invariably asked had to do with personal and social change and with the women's perceptions of themselves and the community. I made followup tapes when they became necessary for clarification. I maintained friendly contact with the subjects of most of the interviews; in a few instances the women had left the community. In general, the information on the tapes—the subjective reality of the women—was the source of my understanding of the community.

Finally, a note about the organization of the body of the work might be helpful. This book is about a community of liberated lesbian-feminists and the influence of lesbian-feminist ideology on their lives. To promote an understanding of the phenomenon, it is necessary to establish conditions that existed before the liberation movements that affected their lives, for comparative purposes. Therefore, the first two chapters delineate attitudes about lesbianism held by the larger culture, and contain a brief history of social change, bringing the reader to the present. The next three chapters focus on various aspects of community life, indicating how these are influenced by lesbian-feminist ideology and how, in the process of developing a community, the ideology itself is modified.

More specifically, what follows in this chapter is a selective overview of the literature related to lesbianism in various fields. Chapter two, a distillation of reading plus discussion with community members, is a brief history of social change, which begins with the development of negative attitudes about homosexuality held by major institutions in our culture, shifts to a description of "old gay life" within this context, continues with the development of social and educational homophile self-help organizations, and concludes with an account of the various liberation movements and their influence on the development of the community.

The next three chapters, which draw heavily from fieldwork and interviews, document aspects of community life. Chapter three is an ethnographic overview of the community. Chapter four looks at social organizations by examining more closely the process by which two community projects were developed within the framework of a lesbian-feminist ideology. Chapter five shifts the focus from the general lesbian-feminist community to a special group within it, lesbian mothers. It describes how lesbian-feminism influenced the techniques lesbian mothers have developed to cope with their situation and with the socialization of their children. Finally, there is a brief summary and an expansion of some of the elements of world view which have emerged from the data.

Review of the Literature

A recurring theme in a study of lesbianism in which the experience and perception of the women themselves are taken into account is the wide divergence between concepts about lesbianism in the literature commonly held by heterosexual "authorities" and the subjective experience and self-definition of the women who are the subject of this research. Unfortunately, it is often the stereotypes generated from research by outsiders that directly affect the lives of the women involved. Such assumptions about homosexuality—that it is caused by "degeneration of genes," that it is a "moral sin," or more recently, a "psychological sickness"—affect the behavior of the outside world toward the lesbian and, more seriously, often affect the lesbian's own feelings about herself as somehow "unnatural" and hence unacceptable vis-à-vis the world of the heterosexual.

Until recently most studies of homosexuals were drawn from patient or prison populations; since the assumption was that homosexuality was a "sickness" or a "crime," this population seemed interchangeable with those who simply had not yet come for treatment or been incarcerated. Female homosexuality was thought to be the same kind of phenomenon as male homosexuality; the fact had not yet been recognized that lesbians had been socialized as women, not as homosexuals, and that therefore their behavior patterns were much more like those of heterosexual women than like homosexual men.

Various writers (Martin and Lyon, 1972; Rosen, 1974; Simon and Gagnon, 1967) have speculated about why lesbianism has been overlooked as a topic of research, whereas there have been many publications about male homosexuality. One reason given for this comparative lack of attention is that lesbiansim (and female sexuality in general) is seen as less important than its male counterpart in the psychiatric research that has been done on homosexuality, much of it oriented toward "curing" the individual so that he can function as a "normal" male. Another reason is that, statistically, lesbians have been less likely than male homosexuals to seek psychiatric treatment and are often less visible than males, both in appearance and behavior. Though there are some exceptions, there is still a dearth of material on nonpatient lesbian attitudes and behavior.

Most research on homosexuality has been published in three areas: psychiatrically oriented material including physiological data (Rosen, 1974); sociological material, usually of the "homosexual as deviant" nature (Gagnon and Simon, 1967a); and a very few anthropological studies of homosexuality in other cultures (Devereaux, 1937; Landes, 1940). However, as recently as 1966, an article appeared in a major anthropological journal arguing that anthropologists should study homosexual groups in their own culture (Sonenschein, 1966). In 1971 Edward Sagarin, in reviewing sociological studies of sex, pointed out the difficulties in doing such research.

Within the last hundred years, four major kinds of literature concerned themselves with the subject of homosexuality in the Western world. The earliest were the post-Darwinian writings of Europeans, either medical men or travelers, who viewed homosexuality as a "degeneration of the genes" or as a relic from earlier, savage times and still to be found among exotic people in remote places. A small minority felt that homosexuality was a manifestation of a higher, more sensitive form of humanity, but this view was not widely accepted. During this early period, serious efforts were made by Krafft-Ebing, Ellis, and Hirschfeld to compile data based on large numbers of histories.

It was the widespread acceptance of Freudian theory of human development that shifted the emphasis of research into psycho-pathological lines, concentrating on case histories of very small samples rather than on broader social patterns.

The third major influence was the seminal work of Kinsey and his colleagues, whose studies focused on the reported sexual behavior of a large number of subjects rather than on the psychological implications of behavior.

The fourth, and perhaps in some ways the most valid, addition to the body of literature about homosexuality is recent material written by members of the group themselves.

Since an underlying assumption of this work about lesbianism is that it, along with male homosexuality, is simply part of the normal range of human sexuality, and since we are looking at social life, I am excluding psychoanalytic literature from this brief overview. However, for those interested readers, Charlotte Wolff's study, *Love Between Women* (1971), is an example of how psychoanalytic theory about lesbianism is engendered. David H. Rosen's excellent monograph, *Lesbianism: A Study of Female Homosexuality* (1974), reviews the literature of patient and nonpatient studies and concludes, with others, that lesbianism is "not a clinical entity." More recently, Barbara E. Sang critically reviewed psychological research on lesbianism (1978) from a lesbian point of view.

To put the phenomenon of lesbian-feminist life into perspective, a selective review of certain kinds of literature is useful. This includes studies of female sexuality, studies of the social life of homosexuals of both sexes, and feminist and lesbian-feminist literature.

Studies of Female Sexuality

The first scientific study of female sexual behavior in America was conducted in 1929 by Katherine Bement Davis, a social worker. It was based on answers from 2,200 women to questionnaires about their sexual experiences and was a precursor to the Kinsey studies to be initiated a decade later. Davis's results showed that half of the single women and one-third of the married women in the study said that they had had "intense emotional relationships" with other women. Based on these data, Davis felt that 10 to 20 percent of all women answering the questionnaire were, at the time, or had once been, homosexual. Her results have been questioned because the sample—college-educated women—was not representative of the total population. Davis may have been naive in accepting answers at face value, unlike the later interviews designed by the Kinsey team in which there were built-in checks, but Davis's work was instrumental in inspiring subsequent studies based on actual sexual behavior. The formation of the Committee for Research on Sex Problems by the National Research Council in 1921, which encouraged many major studies of sex behavior, facilitated this trend.

Stereotypes about the passive nature of female sexuality have been modified as well. Three comprehensive studies indicated that female sexuality is even more intense than male sexuality, that females have simply been socialized to respond with more reticence. These studies are the Kinsey study of female sexual behavior in 1953; research conducted by Masters and Johnson in 1966, in which sexual behavior of males and females during coitus was compared; and Mary Jane Sherfy's work (1966, 1972), which for the first time pulled together data from several disciplines to give a comprehensive picture of the pattern of female sexuality.

One of the implications of the studies was that women did not necessarily need men to have the most effective kinds of sexual experience. Indeed, according to Masters and Johnson (p. 133), the most effective orgasmic technique is automanipulation, the second highest level of erotic intensity results from partner manipulation, and the third highest is orgasm during coitus, though there were those who argued that sexual effectiveness by itself would be rather lonely. However, to lesbians and to some feminists, these findings sustained their view that both sexual and emotional pleasure were most effectively experienced with someone who understood female arousal patterns as well as the need for nurturance and tenderness. The logical choice, based on one line of reasoning, was another female as a partner. (See Nomadic Sisters, *Loving Women*, 1976, for more details on female lovemaking. A glossier approach is Sisley and Harris, *The Joy of Lesbian Sex*, 1977.)

Kinsey and Related Studies

The landmark research on human sexual behavior, and still the best and most thorough, were the two studies of male and female sexual behavior by Alfred Kinsey and his co-workers: *Sexual Behavior in the Human Male* (1948) and *Sexual Behavior in the Human Female* (1953, 1970). These were actually designed as taxonomic studies, descriptions of a species as a result of observing the range of variation in its traits. Great care was taken to avoid skewed samples, and the method of multiple interviewing with built-in checks served to make a high degree of accuracy possible for the first time in studies of human sexual behavior.

The published studies were based on responses from 6,300 white males and 5,300 white females. These findings are especially relevant to the present study: there was a high rate of homosexual behavior in the general population; women's orgasmic capacity was biologically greater than men's; differences in patterns of sexual behavior among men were largely determined by education and occupational levels; among the women the most important factor was decade of birth, not class membership. In regard to homosexuality, it was found that there was no increase in male and female homosexuality decade by decade. As the data were analyzed, Kinsey and his colleagues realized that the actual picture of human sexuality was more complex than simply "heterosexual" or "homosexual" categories. Therefore, they developed a seven-point scale based both on physical acts and on psychological arousal.

The Kinsey findings about lesbianism were that lesbians followed the patterns of women in general, rather than those of homosexual men, in that fewer women had homosexual experiences than men, and those who did have them were less active than men. Only 28 percent of the women had homosexual responses, only 13 percent of those to a peak of orgasm, while 50 percent of the males had physical or emotional responses, 37 percent to an act leading to orgasm (pp. 474–475). Again, following general female rather than homosexual male patterns, lesbians had fewer partners and were more inclined to establish long-term, monogamous relationships than were homosexual men (p. 456.)

Gradually, the realization grew that there are many kinds of homosexualities, just as there are many kinds of heterosexualities. An excellent book, *Sexual Inversion: The Multiple Roots of Homosexuality* (Marmor, 1965), made up of cross-discipline data, warned against the assumption of single-factor causation of homosexuality. However, the focus of this book was still on causation.

Evelyn Hooker's work on male homosexuals in the late 1950s radically modified psychoanalytic assumptions about homosexuality as pathological. She administered projective tests to nonpatient homosexuals (until her study, psychoanalytically oriented studies had used patient populations exclusively) and to a matching sample of heterosexuals. She then asked trained interpreters to these tests to judge the results. They were unable to do so except by chance. The possiblity that homosexuality was not a pathological condition, since indications of pathology did not show up on tests designed for that purpose, was suggested (Hooker, 1957, pp. 18–31). Hooker's pioneer work inspired two similar studies on nonpatient lesbians (Armon, 1960, and Hopkins, 1969) in which it was suggested that not only did lesbians show nonneurotic patterns, they might also be better adjusted than a matching sample of heterosexual women. A more recent psychological study indicated that lesbianism is a "healthy lifestyle," that " the only way most lesbians differ from the majority of the population is in their choice of love object" (Rosen, 1974).

Hooker's work with nonpatient male homosexuals also led her to do a short ethnographic study of a male homosexual community in 1965. A similar though more limited study had been conducted in 1963 by Maurice Leznoff and William Westley on an urban Canadian community in which closeted and noncloseted male homosexuals interacted.

Utilizing the Kinsey data, John H. Gagnon and William Simon of the Institute for Sex Research made a series of studies in the 1960s that supplemented the Kinsey material on homosexuality and concentrated on the *social* life of homosexuals, rather than on etiology (Gagnon and Simon, 1967a; Simon and Gagnon, 1967a; 1967b). Their work helped to shift the perspec-

17

tive away from the concept of homosexuality as "exotic behavior" to more balanced studies of the coping techniques of a minority group and of homosexual community life.

A few popularized studies of lesbianism in America have been published by male authors. Two of the most widely read are *Lesbianism in America* (1965), compiled by Donald Cory, himself a homosexual, and *The Grapevine* (1964), by Jess Stearn, whose book had "if only they knew better" overtones. The time was ripe for lesbians themselves to write about their own experiences. An early scientific attempt was the report in September 1959 of a survey conducted by the San Francisco chapter of the Daughters of Bilitis, which was based on replies to questionnaires sent to readers of their publication, the *Ladder*. The results indicated that lesbians were more conservative and were more interested in long-term relationships than was assumed by the general public, who tended to equate lesbianism with male homosexuality and its more general emphasis on frequent and informal sexual experience. However, their focus was on demonstrating the respectability of the lesbian, and the readership of the article was limited.

Feminist Writings

A major influence in reconstructing the thinking of lesbians—as well as women in general—about themselves were feminist writings that described the crippling effects of the oppression of women as a group by men as a group. The oppression and stigmatization of the lesbian because of her sexual and affectional orientation was defined as part of the general oppression of women by men in a patriarchal culture, and especially of women who did not need to relate to men in their personal lives. The following feminist and lesbian-feminist literature has been cited by members of the group as being most influential: Simone de Beauvoir, *The Second Sex* (1949, 1953); Betty Friedan, *The Feminine Mystique* (1963); Kate Millett, *Sexual Politics* (1969); Shulamith Firestone, *The Dialectic of Sex* (1970); Radicalesbians, *The Woman-Identified Woman* (1970); and the anthology edited by Robin Morgan, *Sisterhood Is Powerful* (1970).

Lesbian-Feminist Material

The impact of various liberation movements led to the publication of works by lesbians writing about their own experience.

A general and thorough overview of the lesbian experience by two women long active in civil rights for lesbians and women is *Lesbian/Woman* by Del Martin and Phyllis Lyon (1972), cited earlier. It is indicative of the controversial nature of this book that the original publisher turned down the final manuscript because the authors did not end the book by rejecting their lesbianism—rather they strongly affirmed it. A similar book on the lesbian experience by two other lesbian partners is *Sappho Was a Right-On Woman: A Liberated View of Lesbianism*, by Sidney Abbott and Barbara Love (1972). Jill Johnston's *Lesbian Nation*, published the following year, contained a series of articles she had written in her column in the *Village Voice*, in which she publicly came out as a lesbian and articulated some of her feelings and experiences resulting from this disclosure.

Fiction about Lesbianism by Female Authors

Novels written by female authors about lesbians appeared as early as 1788. In that year Mary Wollstonecraft's novel *Mary, a Fiction* was published and was said to be based on the author's attachment to another woman, which began when Mary was about fifteen and continued until the woman's death twelve years later (Martin and Lyon, 1972, p. 21).

The classic work for several decades about a lesbian relationship was Radclyffe Hall's *The Well of Loneliness*, published in 1928. It depicted the life of two upper-class English women who were in love with each other. Its publication caused a scandal. However, since the novel sensitively depicted the protagonists and their feelings for each other, it was for many years the most influential book for isolated young lesbians who had no other role models.

Colette also wrote sketches of literary and artistic women she had known in the early part of the century in France. But her sketches depicted rather exotic behavior and so were remote from the experience of many of her readers.

Though there were some novels published in the 1950s and 1960s, most notably *The Price of Salt* by Claire Morgan (1952), not until 1969 was a lyrically romantic novel about a lesbian relationship published in America; its readers were general and widespread. This was *Patience and Sarah*, by Isabel Miller, which was based on the lives of an American primitive painter of the early 1800s and her lover, who settled on a farm in New

York together and lived happily for many years. What is characteristic of this book is both the tenderness between the women and the self-sufficiency of the life they made for themselves. An autobiographical book, in which the author's lesbian relationships are a part of a creative, tumultuous time in her life, is Kate Millett's intensely personal book, *Flying* (1974).

Finally, in 1973, a new kind of book about a funny, intrepid heroine who happens to be a lesbian, Rita Mae Brown's *Rubyfruit Jungle*, was published by a feminist press. A review in the *Lesbian Tide* described the book:

> What is important about Brown's work is that it is the first of its kind. The first published novel that portrays a lesbian as a person. . . . It's not a story about "a Lesbian." It is a story about an unusually strong and colorful woman's irrepressible, funny, and politically personal march through class, sex, and race bigotry while retaining a positive self-image. Brown has written the first contemporary fiction in which a character's lesbian sexuality is an extension rather than a controlling factor of her personality. . . . (Cordova, 1973, *The Lesbian Tide,* p. 19)

Reference Works

Within the last few years, several books have been published which serve as valuable reference works in the area of human sexuality and homosexuality. These books are inclined to view homosexuality nonjudgmentally and to focus on documenting it historically and, in some cases, to indicate how strongly attitudes toward it are affected by cultural context. The Kinsey study on human female sexual behavior was the first to put the range of actual behavior into a broad historical and scientific context. The Kinsey books also included a comprehensive bibliography, which later was published in part in annotated form by the Institute for Sex Research and edited by Martin Weinberg and Alan P. Bell (1972).

Two recent studies of sexual variance put into historical context are *Sexuality and Homosexuality,* by Arno Karlen (1971), and *Sexual Variance in Society and History,* by Vern L. Bullough (1976). A work limited to male homosexuality, but which puts the phenomenon into a cross-cultural and cross-species context, is *Homosexual Behavior Among Males*, by Wainwright Churchill (1967).

A few much-needed research tools have been compiled by dedicated professionals to aid in the development of the field. An important early contribution is Jeannette Foster's *Sex Variant Women in Literature*, which was originally published in 1956 at the author's expense but was reprinted in 1975 by a feminist press. Two more recent bibliographies are *The Lesbian in Literature* (Damon and Stuart, 1975) and *Women Loving Women* (Kuda, 1974). The Task Force on Gay Liberation of the American Library Association issues an excellent, periodically revised bibliography of literature about homosexuality in various areas, and *Heresies*, a New York-based feminist publication, is building a Lesbian Herstory Archives in New York City. The most comprehensive resource book on lesbianism to date is *Our Right to Love: a Lesbian Resource Book* (Vida, 1978) which was produced in cooperation with the women of the National Gay Task Force.

With an eye toward making public the past contributions of homosexuals, a short but detailed work illuminating a little-publicized phenomenon, the homosexual rights movement begun in the last century, *The Early Homosexual Rights Movement, 1864-1953*, by John Lauritsen and David Thorstad, was published in 1974. In the same vein but on a much broader scale is the reissue of the fifty-four volumes of classic, out-of-print works on aspects of homosexuality, edited by Jonathan Katz (1975), and more recently, Katz's comprehensive *Gay American History* (1976).

Yet, in the academy, with few exceptions, studies of lesbian behavior, if conducted at all, still largely focus on such deviant and statistically uncharacteristic settings as prisons (Giallombardo, 1966). The time is long past due for more enlightened attitudes about homosexuality to be routinely incorporated into research designs so that the "everyday reality" of the majority of this group can be documented. When this happens, it will be possible to counteract the negative stereotypes that still underlie research on homosexuality conducted by biased or misinformed heterosexual researchers.

Introduction

Previous Studies

This ethnographic description of an urban lesbian-feminist community draws in part on work done in the past. Evelyn Hooker's pioneer study of a male homosexual community (1962) serves as a pattern on which to build, as do the later Simon and Gagnon studies, which focused on the "nonexotic" group behavior of lesbians. Previous works centered on the San Francisco homosexual community, though focusing largely on males, were used for comparative purposes historically. These are a detailed description of the homosexual bar by Nancy B. Achilles (1964), and Roxanna Sweet's analysis of homophile organizations as part of a social movement (1968). A more recent description, by Elizabeth Barnhart (1975), of an Oregon community shows lesbians incorporating counterculture values. These last two studies describe the beginnings of change, both in attitudes and in social behavior, from old gay life.

The present work describes a significant shift in lesbian self-image and lifestyle as a result of the influence of the women's and gay liberation movements during the late 1960s and early 1970s. It focuses on how the ideology of the liberation movements was incorporated and transformed into action and how this process changed the expectations and self-image of those involved in it.

2. SOCIO-HISTORICAL BACKGROUND

For an understanding of the liberated lesbian community documented in this book, a detailed account of the various epochs of lesbian life and the forces that influenced the development of the community should be set forth. This chapter will describe the major shifts in the nature of the lesbian community. These shifts represent three stages of development: (1) "old gay life," (2) norm-oriented self-help organizations of the 1950s, and (3) the developing community built on lesbian feminist principles.

So that social trends can be properly delineated, a detailed description of "old gay life" (a term widely used by members of the group to denote gay life before liberation), centering around the bars, serves as the baseline for comparison of subsequent change. The texture of old gay life as it emerges from subjective descriptions was filled with secrecy and fear, and was focused on coming to terms with a stigmatized identity.

The process of identifying oneself to oneself and others as a lesbian, known as "coming out," from the term "to come out of the closet," was the first step in self-recruitment to gay life. Once aware of one's lesbian identity, the next step was often the search for a community of others like oneself. The most prominent place to find other lesbians was the gay bar, in which severely dichotomized social roles were assigned and reinforced. Many "old gay" women remember having to choose which role they would play in the lesbian community, and how they learned to play these roles. Most have said that they felt there was no alternative open to them at the time.

The main arena in which lesbian social life was played out was the lesbian bar; therefore a detailed description of the more salient aspects of bar life are included. Because of the nature of the stigmatization that the women faced, and because the function of the place available to them socially was to sell alcohol, many women remember bar life as lonely or fraught with sexual innuendo, jealousy, and possessiveness, sometimes culminating in violence. The underlying reason for the despair experienced by many who took part in old gay life was that the participants had, by and large, accepted the negative stereotype of lesbianism held by the larger culture and therefore felt that this largely depressed lifestyle was what they, as lesbians, deserved.

The next socio-historical era in the evolution of lesbian life was the homophile organization of the 1950s, whose function was to help change the attitude of both society and the lesbian toward the implications of lesbianism. This was done, however, within the context of the norms of the larger society. The process focused on education, appropriate research, socializing in a group context as an alternative to the bars, and working for common goals in coalitions with other groups. The major lesbian organization from 1955 through the late 1960s was the Daughters of Bilitis, of which a detailed account will be given to permit a valid comparison with the social organizations that followed the liberation movements.

The third stage represents not a gradual cultural change but a jarring shift in goals, tactics, and rationale. The primary catalysts for such change were the various liberation movements: women's liberation, gay liberation, and from these the emergence of militant lesbian-feminism. The new focus was on a proud, positive definition of lesbians as the vanguard of a feminist future, and on a demand for a basic reconstruction of both self and society.

The present study is limited to the emerging lesbian-feminist community in San Francisco. It does not include the many women who live in San Francisco who are lesbians but are not lesbian-feminists. The implications of lesbian-feminism and how it influences both the long-range projects of the community and its daily life will be made clear through a detailed description of how aspects of the women's and gay liberation movements contributed to its development.

Old Gay Life and the Beginnings of Change

If we are to understand the dynamics of old gay life, it must be seen against the wider background of the repressive attitudes and practices of the major institutions of the larger culture. This section briefly describes the historical development of the negative attitudes toward homosexuality as practiced by the church, the law, the psychiatric profession, and as a result of these, often by the parents of the lesbian, and to some degree, the lesbian herself.

Subjective History

For many contemporary lesbian informants, their collective social history is roughly divided into several epochs. The Golden Age in the distant past was seen by many lesbians as a time dimly remembered and imperfectly documented because of the vested interests of male-patriarchal historians. The Golden Age included such symbols of the strength of the female principle as worship of the Mother Goddess, a matriarchal and therefore harmonious culture, the great tribe of women warriors the Amazons, and the historical figure of the famous poet and intellectual whose name has been closely identified with the flowering of lesbianism at its highest point, Sappho of Lesbos. That golden epoch ended with the rise of patriarchal Judeo-Christian traditions in which Mother-worship was superseded by the one male godhead, and the role of women and of lesbians became subordinate to men.

For lesbians who are rediscovering and reinterpreting their history, there were two other periods in which, for a little while, what has been identified by them as lesbian activity again surfaced, but was quickly repressed. The period of about 1300–1700 in Europe was looked upon by some as a time of martyrdom for women healers who were secret followers of the Mother cult and who were burned as witches by the church. Many of the estimated nine million women who were burned were said to be lesbians, and it was this difference from the norm which led to their being accused of witchcraft.

A more recent period was the early part of this century, in which a particular group of women identified themselves as lesbians, or in some cases as bisexual, and publicly led colorful and creative lives. Flaunting the end of Victorian repression, women of means or of artistic ability congregated—many in liaisons with other women—and because of their privileged position were allowed to do so with little censure. To many, they represented a new kind of freedom. Gertrude Stein and Alice B. Toklas, Romaine Brooke, Vita Sackville-West, and Colette were part of such groups in England and on the continent.

But the more usual reality for recent generations of lesbians in America was bleak decades during which most of them experienced oppression, potential arrest and exposure, and an internalized view of lesbianism as a social stain. The only public place to socialize with other lesbians, if one dared risk periodic arrests, was the gay bar, even though bar life was not comfortable for many women. Because major institutions in American life helped to perpetuate the view of the lesbian as, at best, an undesirable "deviant," many women had no recourse but to develop behavior patterns typical of social "deviants." The institutions included the church, which defined "deviant sexual behavior" as sinful; the law, which saw it as illegal; the psychiatric profession, to whom it was "sick"; and finally, strongly influenced by the first three, many families of homosexuals who felt that their homosexual members were shameful. With all these sources of disapproval engendering and reinforcing a negative self-image of the emerging lesbian, and with very real retribution confronting her, it is no wonder that the social self that has been described by most women was, at best, an uncomfortable one in which many areas of natural self-expression had to be ruthlessly repressed. The following sections briefly describe the background for religious, legal, and psychiatric rejection of homosexuality.

The Judgments of Religion

What kind of self-image has the church given the Lesbian? Less than human, sinner, celibate, unworthy, evil-minded, accursed, wicked, impure. (Martin and Lyon, 1972, p. 34).

Though there are a few, often cited excerpts from the Scriptures, mostly from Leviticus, denouncing male homosexuality, there is only one reference, and it is in the New Testament (Romans 1:26), which describes the "vile affection" of women for each other as being "against nature."

The church originally defined homosexuality as "sinful" for two reasons: it was not procreative, and it was associated with paganism. There are historical reasons for this attitude. To the small tribe of ancient Hebrews, procreation was essential for their survival as a people. Not only was homosexuality a threat to survival because it decreased the number of children born to members of the tribe, it was also considered an "abomination" because homosexual practices were associated with pagan rites. Therefore, in order to delineate the Israelites from their pagan neighbors, not only was intermarriage proscribed, but so were practices associated with pagan rites and with their own pre-Mosaic past, such as worshipping the golden calf at Mount Sinai, and homosexuality.

The strong sense that homosexuals are "sinful" has persisted to the present day, denying homosexuals one traditional source of comfort and support in our culture—established religion, which has made a practice of excluding known homosexuals. Because of this, many women to whom religion was an important part of their lives were forced to abandon their active affiliation with the religion in which they had been raised. Many women have said that the awareness that they were lesbians caused them the greatest suffering in the sphere of religion because they expected to be denied salvation. Some still attend traditional church services, but in a closeted condition, where they hear, as a part of the church liturgy, periodic denunciations of homosexuality.

The Sanctions of the Law

The strong moral stance taken by both the law and the traditional church against homosexuality has its roots in the time when church and state were one. In America today, both legal assumptions and practices, as well as religious interdictions, stem from the strong influence of English common law on the legal system, and from Judeo-Christian concepts of morality, strongly laced with the Calvinism of our Founding Fathers, in the religous sphere (Churchill, 1967, p. 203). In the rule of Justinian (527–547) during a series of natural disasters which he believed were the result of God's punishing "abominations against nature", homosexuals were killed en masse, "lest as a result of these impious acts, whole cities would perish together with their inhabitants" (p. 204). As Churchill indicates:

The laws against homosexual behaviour that were devised at the beginning of the Christian State established a precedence not only by interdicting such behaviour under any and all conditions and making it a matter for public concern, but also by punishing it to great excess. These same tendencies are reflected in all subsequent anti-homosexual legislation. (p. 205)

By the Middle Ages, sodomy had become equated with heresy and witchcraft as well as treason. The reasoning was this: "Anyone who would practice pagan love is a heretic, all heretics and witches attempt to subvert authority of both Church and State and are therefore traitors" (p. 205).

Not until centuries later, with the introduction of the Napoleonic Code in 1810, which was influenced by the social and political reforms sweeping through Europe in the eighteenth century, were laws against homosexual behavior between consenting adults in private dropped from the books. Similar reforms were adopted in all Western countries except England, Germany, and America.

The Legal Situation in America

There appears to be no other major culture in the world in which public opinion and the statute law so severely penalize homosexual relationships as they do in the United States today. (Kinsey, 1953, p. 483)

State and municipal laws against homosexual behavior vary from place to place. Homosexual acts may be prosecuted as "sodomy," "oral copulation," "anal intercourse," "infamous crimes against nature," or "lascivious acts." Many of these illegal acts apply to normal lovemaking practices by heterosexuals, but they are almost uniformly enforced only against homosexuals (Churchill, 1967, p. 225). The penalties of such acts also vary, from felonies in most states to misdemeanors in others. Punishments also range from small fines to life imprisonment. In Georgia, for example, life imprisonment is mandatory for sodomy unless clemency has been recommended (Karlen, 1971, p. 609).

Not only is there severe anti-homosexual legislation and a policy of harassment in putting these laws into practice, there is

28

also severe discrimination against homosexuals in both federal and state jobs, in the armed forces, in consistent judgments against lesbian mothers as "unfit," in housing, in employment, and in general ostracism. As Churchill states:

> It may be justly claimed that a person of known homosexual persuasion or even a person merely suspected of homosexual inclinations is likely to suffer common abuse as well as abridgement of his human rights in the United States more often and in many more ways than a member of any other minority. Moreover, when he is abused and deprived of his rights as a citizen and as a human being, he is less likely than a member of even the most harassed religious or racial minority to obtain the support of any other individual or group. (p. 219)

In recent years there has been a shift in attitude especially among experts in the fields of law, medicine, religion, and psychiatry concerning anti-homosexual laws. In 1962, Illinois became the first state to make adult consensual homosexuality legal. By 1976, sixteen states had such laws, among them California. State Assemblyman Willie Brown, Jr., had introduced a bill repealing all laws regulating sexual conduct between consenting adults in private in every legislative session since 1969. In January 1976, it finally became state law in California.

There is not now and there never has been a law in America against lesbianism as such. This situation is attributed to Queen Victoria, who, according to folklore, was said to exclaim: "Two *ladies* would never engage in such despicable acts!" when an advisor inquired whether women were to be included in the new laws being enacted against male homosexuality. (Martin and Lyon, p. 42) Since American laws concerning sexual practices are heavily influenced by English common laws, the attitude of taking lesbianism less seriously than male homosexuality pertained in America. The only area in which women are more consistently and heavily penalized by the courts for lesbianism is in custody cases involving lesbian mothers (see chapter five).

Yet, though lesbians, aside from an occasional raid on a bar, faced arrest much less frequently than homosexual men, the knowledge that they *could* be arrested on some charge related to their affectional orientation resulted in the development of protective anxiety. Even the suspicion of lesbianism had very real consequences in the lives of many women who were defined as "undesirable" and therefore lost their jobs, were evicted from their homes, had their children taken away, were dishonorably dismissed from the armed forces, and in other ways were discriminated against. Because many of them had accepted society's negative definition of homosexuality, they felt they had no recourse.

The Attitudes of Psychology

As science replaced religion as the purveyor of truth to many in our culture, the field of psychology postulated a more "enlightened" view of homosexuality, to wit, that it was not a "sin" after all, it was a "sickness," and as such, it could be cured. Some of the "cures" were extreme: the use of electric shock and clitorectomies to treat lesbianism is not unknown.

Characteristically, most early psychological studies assumed that homosexuality was, by definition, a pathological condition, since until the Hooker study (1957) all work had been conducted on patient populations. Given the assumption of pathology, the professional imperative was to find the "cause" of homosexuality so that the budding homosexual could be spotted early in life and treated, and that conditions thought to encourage homosexuality could be contended with.

Psychoanalysts such as Sigmund Freud, Ernest Jones, and Helene Deutsch suggested various "causes" of lesbianism based on individual analysis of female homosexual patients.[1] These ranged from "pronounced penis envy," "orality and sadism," "castration complex," to—a favorite—"overidentification with the mother coupled with a weak father im-

1. The view held by the present writer and others (Martin and Lyon, 1972; Simon and Gagnon, 1971) is that homosexuality is simply one part of the spectrum of human sexuality; therefore, to look for causality is to reinforce an underlying pathological assumption. However, for those readers who are interested in literature on etiology, Rosen covers the subject nicely (1974, pp. 70–71). There he cites Martin and Lyon, who state that "we tend to feel that persons are born sexual; not heterosexual or homosexual, just sexual. And the direction a girl's sexuality may take depends upon her individual circumstances and life experiences, and how she reacts to them." Rosen agrees with Kinsey that the nature of the first sexual experience seems to be influential in subsequent affectional preference.

age." Martin and Lyon list fifty-four of these "causes" suggested by professionals, all based on patient populations. They point out that the underlying assumption made by the psychoanalytic profession about homosexuals is that they have a "psycho-physiological predisposition to be mentally aberrant" (pp. 48–49).

Even if the young lesbian did not have direct contact with members of the helping professions, often their literature defining her lifestyle as a "perversion" had a strong, negative influence on her life. Many women describe the process of gradually realizing that they were lesbians in isolation, of feeling that because of a lack of role models they were the only one in the world "like this," and of finally coming upon medical or psychoanalytic literature reflecting the norms of the larger culture in which a "scientific" description of homosexuality as pathological could only depress them and cause deep anxiety.

As more became known about a nonpatient population of homosexuals, and with the visibility of a population of more activist homosexuals, even the august American Psychiatric Association removed homosexuality from its list of diagnostic disorders in 1973. New schools of therapy—humanistic, feminist, radical—have defined homosexuality not as aberrant behavior but rather as a viable lifestyle, part of the range of normal human sexuality. They have counseled clients to affirm their homosexuality instead of trying to change it. Many lesbian-feminists, however, prefer to use problem-solving groups made up of other lesbians who share similar experiences and have a first-hand knowledge of some of the common problems; or, if they are counseled on a one-to-one basis, prefer a lesbian or at least a feminist therapist.

Families of Origin

Many lesbians have said that it is with their own parents that they find it most difficult to share the knowledge of their affectional orientation. Many women are successfully integrated into the lesbian community, are in long-term relationships with women they love, openly identify themselves as lesbians without constraint—and still find that they cannot tell their parents that they are lesbians.

There is some justification for their reticence. Parents are thought by many homosexuals to share the values of preceding generations, to whom the implications of homosexuality were more likely to be both guilt-provoking and shameful. Parents may feel that their daughter is a lesbian because of something that they, as parents, did wrong during her formative years. Daughters often find it difficult to contend with the excessive guilt that parents with these attitudes assume.

Some parents who have discovered their daughter's lesbianism have reacted in extreme ways. Some women have been taken out of school by their parents, sent to psychiatrists, even put into mental institutions. Other women have had their parents pray for them, that they will see the "error of their ways" and repent; some have been excommunicated, or even declared dead by religious parents who cannot correlate their deep loathing of "sexual perversion" with a member of their own family. Again and again women have reported with bewilderment, "But I'm still the same person," only to find that the knowledge of their lesbianism can color for others every other aspect of their lives.

Some women have said that they simply felt it would cause too much complication on the parts of aged or sick parents to have to come to terms with their assumptions about their daughter's lesbianism. Therefore, they choose not to have a direct confrontation, out of consideration for their parents. Other informants say that, although they have never told their parents in so many words that they are lesbians, they know that their parents are probably aware of it. As long as there is no direct confrontation, each side of the relationship can maintain his or her role comfortably.

For the parents who want to understand their daughter's life as a lesbian, organizations are emerging for parents of homosexuals, who meet together and exchange information. One such group was established in San Francisco by William Johnson, an ordained minister and a homosexual, and Phyllis Lyon, co–author of *Lesbian/Woman*. However, few parents as yet know about such organizations or are willing to belong to them.

Thus, to the "old gay" lesbian, the pejorative attitudes of the major institutions in our culture often served to make the realization of her lesbianism a secret, shameful, guilty experience. By denying her validity, these external forces largely defined the limited boundaries of old gay life. And her own acceptance of these attitudes, as part of her socialization as a member of the culture, affected her life in many ways.

Because of the negative attitude toward homosexuality which permeated the culture, it is not surprising that the process of coming to terms with one's lesbianism often involved the development of two social identities: the carefully constructed and self-consciously maintained "closeted" one of heterosexuality for the general public, and the emerging and fragile lesbian identity among one's peers. Many women who became aware of their lesbianism before the liberation movements describe their sense of shame or guilt when they first realized that they might be lesbian and what this implied to them.

Coming Out

The process of "coming out" or unequivocally identifying oneself as a homosexual seems to involve several stages. As it is used by members of the community, the phrase "to come out" indicates that one identifies oneself as a lesbian, but this process is by no means an abrupt occurrence. Rather, in the experience of many informants, it implies gradually realizing that one's feelings about women are much deeper and more emotional and erotic than feelings about men; becoming aware that this is a manifestation of being a lesbian; coming to terms with the social role and its implications; and finally, publicly committing some act that irrevocably identifies one, to oneself and informed others, as a lesbian. In some cases the symbolic act has been going to a lesbian bar; wearing a button with an appropriate slogan (Dyke, Gay and Proud, ♀, I'm a Lesbian and I'm Beautiful, are current examples); marching in a political parade or taking part in a demonstration as a member of the group; actively looking for another woman as a lover; or finally, having a sexual experience with another woman.

The process of coming out also consists of communicating to non-lesbians that one is a lesbian—for example, "I came out to the head of my department," "I finally came out to my parents." With each contact with people from her former life, as well as with the unaware with whom she may presently have contact, the process of coming out entails a decision of how much to reveal and to whom.

Denise Cronin, in *Coming out Among Lesbians* (1974), points out that the process generally falls into one of two patterns. A woman gradually realizes over a period of time that she has the appropriate romantic feelings according to the expectations of her culture, but for the *inappropriate* sex—her own; or she is unaware that she could have special feelings for women until she falls in love with another woman, sometimes through a process of "romantic drift," beginning with "close mutual friendship and a gradual progression to sexuality" (pp. 270–271), and realizes that the depth of these feelings are far more profound than those previously experienced with men. In actuality, some women who consider themselves lesbians have never had a physical relationship with another woman; most of these are older, closeted women, some are celibate by choice, others are married to men. To be a lesbian does not always involve the process of coming out to others.

The pattern of lesbian sexuality resembles more closely that of heterosexual women than of either homosexual or heterosexual men in that an awareness of and a commitment to their homosexuality generally occurs later for lesbians than for homosexual men (Gagnon and Simon, 1967b, p. 251). According to Gagnon and Simon, lesbians also tend to emphasize the emotional aspects of their relationships in their choosing to establish long-term, stable partnerships; whereas freedom to act on specifically sexual relationships is associated more readily with the behavior of homosexual men (Simon and Gagnon, 1967a).

In the group of women I talked to there seemed to be a common pattern experienced by the women in Cronin's first category, who gradually realized that they were attracted to other women before they were in a relationship with a particular woman. The pattern includes at least some of the following elements: (1) an attraction, sometimes as early as the age of five, to a girl playmate; (2) a strong crush on a female teacher; (3) an awareness of fantasizing romantic scenarios about a specific girlfriend, usually in one's teens; (4) the drabness or "unnaturalness" experienced in trying to date boys and not really wanting to; (5) finally coming across some mention of homosexuality, often vivid and negative, and realizing that one is probably a lesbian; (6) trying to correlate with this realization all the negative stereotypes absorbed from the prevailing culture; and (7) finally coming to terms with it in some way and trying to find others like oneself. As one working-class woman expressed it:

> I came out in different stages. First I came out emotionally. Emotionally, I've always been attached to teachers or had crushes. When I was about eight, a girl—it was just a feeling—she sat next to me one time in class, and my heart started beating really fast, and I thought I was having a heart attack. . . .
>
> Then later I came out mentally, realizing this emotion had a name. . . . I thought I was the only one who felt that way, I felt there was something wrong with me—I went to church a lot, trying to redirect it—I couldn't bear thinking it was physical, it was a *spiritual* union I had with this friend. When I was older I went through the dictionary and found the word "homosexual." I kept looking it up and every thing was with a negative connotation. . . .
>
> Then I came out physically, when I was twenty. I had been compromising my feelings by cultivating these "friendships" when I really wanted more. . . . So I moved into this place where women stayed and I met this woman who I had heard rumors was a lesbian. And I was just *really* curious and just really looked at her all the time—kind of just really wondering how she was different. And I let her see that I was around—she was the only gay person I knew [the narrator invited the woman to see her room and offered her some beer—a gesture of sophistication] and somehow I just *knew* that this was it. . . .
>
> So she drank the beer and I kind of just let it happen, I let her approach me. . . . I felt guilty afterward, but it fulfilled a need in me. It just seemed right. . . .

Later the situation was reversed when the still relatively inexperienced narrator was approached herself by a younger woman who knew she was gay and who wanted to be brought out. The narrator still felt such guilt that, though she cared about the younger woman, she made her write a note to the effect that she wouldn't blame the narrator or feel guilty afterward.

So I made her repeat the words: "It is by my will that I am sleeping with X and I won't feel guilty afterwards." She was a virgin and I didn't know that and I said "You didn't tell me and I feel terrible. Most lesbians have already been with men. Are you sure? Do you *know* that this is what you want?" She said, "Yes. I've always known it, but I've never met anyone." I said, "Then if I'm the first one, I feel used." She said, "No."

I wanted her to come to the point where she told me that she cared about me. We were struggling with it, like it's so hard to say. It was hard for me, too. And even after we got together, it was still hard for me. . . . She'd want me to say it in public. . . . That was her gay reassurance, but I just don't feel like making an exhibition of it. . . . We got along real well. We lasted two years.

Another woman who experienced the second pattern mentioned by Cronin, realizing that she was a lesbian when after a long career of heterosexual dating she drifted into an especially close friendship with another woman, talks about it:

Q: When did you first become aware of your feelings about women?

A: When I was a senior in college, I had one very close friend. And it became clearer and clearer to me that she truly loved me and I loved her, and what love meant, and it really became very evident what *was* missing in my other relationships [with men].

And it happened to be that she was the one who was giving me those responses. . . . And our relationship grew more and more intense during our senior year. . . . And after I graduated we went on a trip together . . . and we finally made love and that was—I was kind of surprised by it, because I was very much into thinking that it was a bad thing, that it was evil, that I wouldn't like it, that two women couldn't make love to each other. . . . But it happened very gradually, we'd hold hands, and then kiss—one night we were kissing and it became a passionate kiss. . . . But it felt fine. And that was the thing that amazed me. The first night that we made love, I felt terrific. It was very, very ecstatic, very, very happy. And I just remember

3. A lesbian couple showing affection. (Laura Wilensky)

going through the day feeling like ... wait a minute, I thought that God would strike me dead, I thought that I was supposed to feel very remorseful, and I was supposed to feel like I had done something very evil. And that wasn't the case at all. I was very elated, and [quietly] it felt very beautiful.... After that year together we thought we would both go and get married, that what had happened between us was just something very unique and very special but not to be continued. It wasn't accepted by society....

And she went off and after she left, I lost twenty pounds, I was walking in mud puddles ... I became very depressed, I wasn't ready. In no way did I prepare myself for that kind of separation anxiety. We were involved in a marriage, and it had been for two years, and we hadn't named it. And in not naming it, we certainly didn't prepare ourselves for the kind of anxiety that would happen when you *stop*.... It was a terribly painful time in my life. And there were just no words. And I didn't know anybody else to talk about it with....

As women became aware that they might be lesbians, they searched for external clues in their own behavior or in that of others. They began to look for what the folklore had taught them about the signs of a lesbian identity. The following items of folklore were discussed in a women's class on lesbianism held at San Francisco State University in the fall of 1973, and at a meeting of the Daughters of Bilitis in San Francisco in the spring of 1973. Many of the women first heard them in grammar and high school. Almost all of them imply that some characteristic physical or behavioral sign will give a lesbian away.

Among the signs are the wearing of certain colors associated with being gay, sometimes only if worn on certain days. The two most often cited were the wearing of green or yellow on Thursday. Some women reported inadvertently putting on these colors and then remembering that it was "Fairy Day" and hastily changing clothes. A color even more strongly associated with being gay and used as such by the gay community itself is lavender. During the lesbian protest in NOW (see p. 64), the women wore lavender T-shirts and referred to themselves as the Lavender Menace in response to Betty Friedan's referring to the issue of lesbianism as a "lavender herring." A reason for the association of lavender with being gay, reported by a lesbian who had been in the gay community for several years, is that "pink is for girls, blue is for boys, so the color in between, lavender, is for homosexuals."

Another practice said to be a sure indication that the wearer is homosexual is the wearing of a ring on the little finger, a "pinkie ring." Most recently, both lesbians and gay men have also worn one pierced-ear ring as a similar kind of self-identification.

Women who wore lumber jackets, had short, male-type haircuts, wore men's undergarments—in short, the old stereotype of how a "bull-dyke," an exceptionally masculine-appearing lesbian, dresses—are also thought to be signifying that they are lesbians. The writer was once walking with a lesbian who had short hair and was wearing a blue workshirt, levis, and motorcycle boots, when one of a group of adolescent boys yelled at her: "Are you a man or a woman?" She replied: "I'm more man than you'll ever be and more woman than you'll ever be able to handle!" There was no reply.

There are other indications besides dress and adornment. Among these are body movements. Some of the most common alleged indications of lesbianism, circulated at high school level are these: if a woman holds her books at her side rather than in front of her "as girls do," if she looks at her fingernails with the palm facing her and the fingers bent, and if she walks "like a man" with long strides. In reality, in the lesbian community, indications of being a lesbian, especially with other lesbians, are much more subtle combinations of body movement, dress, prolonged eye contact, and social context—being where lesbians are expected to be.

Many women at first may feel that they are "not real lesbians" because they themselves don't match the stereotype of what a lesbian is or does. Other women feel that they are not "real" lesbians, especially if they are relating to both men and women; rather they are bisexuals.[2] Until a woman has found a community, or at least has found a lover and a minimal social network to which to attach herself, she often keeps testing herself to see if she really is a lesbian. One woman explains:

It's by your second relationship [with a woman]—your first, you say: "That's just souls loving souls, my unique way of expressing love to that woman." And the second time it happens, you figure there's something more going on. I found more women that I was attracted to than men. And that made a difference. Then I started saying that I was bisexual. Then I remember one gay guy coming up to me and saying that everyone is built bisexual in that you can get sexual pleasure from either sex. *But* when you walk down the street you are attracted to one sex more than the other. And that's true for most people, he said. And I did the test. [Laughs] I walked down this one college street, and he was right! I really did notice women! So then I thought that must mean that I'm a lesbian.

2. It is here that recent political ideology has played a role. In Europe, according to several women visiting San Francisco, bisexuality is "chic," and it is assumed that people in certain upper-class or bohemian circles are bisexual. However, in America among many political lesbians, bisexuality is regarded as a betrayal, since it is as a *lesbian* that one is persecuted. Therefore, it is felt, the politically correct thing is to define oneself as a lesbian, not as a bisexual, and to choose not to relate to men, since men are seen as oppressors of women. More recently, however, support groups for bisexual women have been formed, since affectional orientation may not be so easily submerged.

Socio-historical Background

Role-playing

Not only did lesbians find that, once they acknowledged their lesbianism, their social world was vastly restricted, they also often found that in the gay world as well there were limited role possibilities. In general, and most strongly in the bars—often the first point of contact with the lesbian community for the new lesbian—the old gay world divided up into "butch" and "femme," an approximation of the heterosexual male and female social roles. Butches were tough, presented themselves as being as masculine as possible—with male clothing, sometimes extending to breast-binding and male underwear—and they assumed the traditional male role of taking care of their partners, even fighting over them if necessary, providing for them financially, and doing the "men's" jobs around the house. Femmes, by contrast, were protected, ladylike, attractive in the way that is often described as "cute" or "pretty," sometimes accentuating their appearance, in contrast to their partners, with makeup, elaborate hair styles, and frilly kinds of clothing. They cooked, cleaned house, and took care of their "butch." The roles were sharply delineated in public, and this role-maintenance often carried over in private, sometimes extending to techniques of lovemaking—in some cases the butch would only initiate lovemaking and not allow herself to be touched (Martin and Lyon, 1972:72).[3]

Several reasons have been postulated for the kinds of role-playing especially prevalent in the bar culture in the lesbian community. The major one is that lesbians, raised in a heterosexually-oriented culture, where the male-female paradigm is the appropriate pattern for love relationships, have no other role models available. It has been suggested, as well, that role-playing is more prevalent among working-class lesbians, who are thought to have experienced stronger role adher-

3. Many feminists point out that such extreme role-playing was patterned after and paralleled the exaggerated and limited roles available to heterosexual couples before the widespread reassessment of role expectation engendered by the women's movement and adopted by both women and men, whatever their affectional orientation. Thus, egalitarian relationships as a more current model are not restricted to the lesbian community but are indicative of broader cultural change. However, they do throw the strict role dichotomy in old gay life into proper perspective, in that heterosexual couples were behaving that way too.

ence in their own blue-collar families. As the majority of women who frequent the bars are of working-class origin, this social pattern is reinforced (Abbott and Love, p.94; Martin and Lyon, p.77).

Butch roles are also often more strongly assumed by young women who are newly aware of their lesbianism and are looking for a community. They may dress in a more extreme manner, patterned after the heterosexual stereotype of the "bull-dyke," in order to be recognizable as lesbians. They may, as well, be experimenting with the texture of a new social role. Abbott and Love explain:

> Since the bar is usually the point of entry into the gay subculture, the Lesbian is often unsure of her identity and is susceptible to new images. She knows nothing about who she is or who she's supposed to be as a Lesbian and is ripe for socialization by the subculture. . . . she tries to be a good Lesbian, emulating the practiced Lesbians she meets. . . . She cannot afford to be excluded here; it is her last chance. She puts on the right costume, develops certain attitudes and gestures and the right language. (p. 96)

A few women who have played the butch role have felt that they were really "a man in a woman's body." It has been suggested that this attitude was functional in adjusting to the guilt of acting out a stigmatized social role (Martin and Lyon, p. 73). Abbot and Love found that most "old gay" women felt, however that they had few options.

> Most human beings seem more secure and content if the content and obligations of their relationships are clearly spelled out. . . . Lesbians compromise their identity to be accepted in the traditional gay culture. . . . Even if both women in a Lesbian relationship appear feminine (or masculine), the "old bar culture" . . . might try to separate them into butch and femme, depending on which one performs more duties usually reserved for one sex or the other. (pp. 92–93)

In the Lesbian bar particularly butch and femme roles function as expectations that the young woman tries to live up to. Often she chooses arbitrarily whether to appear butch or femme. If she hesitates or refuses to make a choice, she is seen as "ki-ki," which means pejoratively that she plays both roles. In the old bar culture few women are interested in a woman with a "confused identity." Lesbians confronted with a ki-ki may feel the same difficulty as heterosexual men and women who may not be sure if they are talking to a male or a female. The attitude in the bar is that any woman who is ki-ki is almost impossible to relate to. (pp. 93–94)

One "old gay" informant describes her experience in seeking out the lesbian community as being pressured into choosing a role and finally evolving out of it:

It was 1960 . . . and something inside of me finally said: "I want to meet them." So I went to the ballpark, the place where lesbians play softball, and I had hair clear down to my butt, and I had levis and a sweatshirt on and because I didn't have short hair but yet I had butch clothes on, they were very suspicious of me and I had to go to bed with one of them and then have her brag about it around to have them accept me as a lesbian. . . . Then, all of a sudden, I was a very popular butch. I was forced into the role—they decided I was butch because I was aggressive and strong and could fight and because [pause] I, too, decided I was a butch. *There were only two categories available to me* [my stress] and I knew I wasn't a femme. And I wasn't turned on when butches aggressed me, so I had to be a butch. . . .

I found out that it was the facade I presented as a super-neat butch who would protect them, the whole male role thing, that really turned them on, so I cut my hair shorter and I started wearing T-shirts under my shirt and did the whole trip, and every once in a while sort of established my position in the community by beating the hell out of somebody. . . . I never initiated a fight, but I was mildly relieved if someone initiated one with me because it gave me a chance to show my skills and establish my position in the community. . . . I was into the butch thing for about two years, heavily into it publicly, *in order not to be ostracized* [my stress], I maintained it. *Personally*, in my interactions, I began to drop away from it. I began to be a woman who loved women.

Q: What are the characteristics of that? As opposed to a butch who loves women?

A: It's just being yourself, a woman. It's not opening doors, it's not lighting cigarettes, it's not protecting. It's not "I'm the butch and I have to be on top." It's not "I'm the butch and I will empty the garbage and you will do the cooking and the dishes." What it is, is "Today I'll do the dishes and tomorrow you do the dishes"—an honest sharing.

Some of the experiences described above show a general pattern. Many women who were defined by the community as butches or femmes, and who learned to play out the role, often did not maintain it privately as they adjusted to living with a lover in a long-term relationship. The strain of maintaining such an extreme role in day-to-day life was too great. After all, the women with whom they were relating did not want a man or to be a man, they wanted a love relationship with another woman, and the personal characteristics of the individual transcended arbitrary role delineations.

Still, in public gay life, women felt that they were pressured into maintaining butch-femme roles and that the maintenance of such roles was one major characteristic of old gay life. The arena for the designation and maintenance of these roles was the one place where lesbians could socialize publicly—the gay bar.

The Gay Bar

The gay bar was the focal point of the old gay community. It was the one place where a woman could be sure of meeting other lesbians, of not having to maintain the closeted role she might have had to present during the day at her job, and of being in a context whose rules she understood and in which she could feel some semblance of a community. It was the place where emerging lesbians often came as their first contact with other lesbians. It served as the place in which arbitration of behavior in the lesbian community was reinforced, and by its nature it was where the butch and femme roles were often introduced and

4. *Two women playing pool in a women's bar. One aspect of old gay life that has carried over. (Virginia Morgan)*

were most strongly adhered to.[4] But basically, as most women characterize the bar, it was a place of acute sexual awareness, a place in which loneliness could be relieved, if only briefly, by drinking and through short-term sexual relationships initiated in the bar.

4. When I showed this section to an active lesbian-feminist who had taken part in old gay life, she amended my perception that old gay life and bar life, except for "closeted" women, were synonymous. "For the millions of lesbians who were doing the bar scene, there were millions more who, though paranoid and oppressed, nevertheless felt good about themselves and even before the movement felt it was *society* who fucked up and not them/us. Not just the gay bars. I remember lots of private parties, lots of covert gathering together in homes to drink and flirt and dance and get jealous and even occasionally talk about literature or ideas or even about being gay. We busted up a lot of cars and drank too much and really tore at each other a lot instead of at the outside world that was making us ghettoized, but those parties were more exciting to

Because of its sexual ambience, the bar was threatening to couples. One of the "games" often played in bars, according to some informants, was trying to take a woman from her lover, as a challenge. Some of the practices in the bars were as oppressive as those in male gay bars or singles bars. Sexual attractiveness, sometimes proved by "scoring," was the coin of exchange; other personal qualifications seemed irrelevant. One woman describes the effect of context in defining the situation. At the time, she was new on the scene and more interested in looking for friends than finding a lover:

> It was hard for me to get across the idea that I really wanted to be friends with people, because in the bar, the whole bar trip, any time you approach anybody to talk to them for a light or anything, it's like right away you're after their body. And it was hard for me to work around that, especially in a bar. And then I realized that there was something about a bar—that people are into the bars for escape and the minute you walk out of the bar, it's altogether different. And so I started learning to walk *out* of the bar with people to start *talking* to them and we could see where we were really at.

Generally, the gay bars were controlled by outside forces: the local police, who could harass or arrest the clientele and the management if they wanted to put pressure on the community; and the Alcoholic Beverage Control Board of California, which has the power to revoke the bar's liquor license if it believes that the bar does not adhere to its rules. It was the responsibility of the owner or bartender to see that proper behavior was observed. Reflecting the norms of the larger culture, the rules for behavior are more stringent for gays than for heterosexuals. For example, kissing and dancing are not prevented in bars if practiced by heterosexuals; they are prohibited in gay bars between

---

me (and I suspect to thousands of women) than any bar could ever be. The bars were too risky. We'd lose our jobs if someone saw us there and ratted on us. But we could get together a lot of friends/lovers/rivals and it was at those gatherings that I experienced my social context of being gay. Furthermore, I went to lots of parties with both women and men—that was perhaps even more common—and a little less riotous. The men partied with us because they, too, wouldn't risk the bars. You should make clear that there were *lots* of us who partied privately as an alternative to the bars."

members of the same sex. The bartender, waitresses, and even other habitués of the bar are quick to warn the offender if behavior becomes too intimate as defined by the board or the police. The reaction of the local police depends partly on the current political situation. In the days before liberation the management and clientele of gay bars—whether male, mixed, or female—were in constant fear of a surprise raid at any time. These raids were defined by the law enforcers as "cleaning up the city"; their purpose was to harass homosexuals. A particular threat to being in a gay bar during a raid was that it was a common, though illegal, practice to inform the families and employers about the nature of the charges.

Partly as a reaction to the threat of outside forces, the owners and some of the staff of the gay bars in San Francisco formed an organization, the Tavern Guild, for mutual support—to share common problems and to work out techniques for dealing with them—and to socialize. One solution to some of their problems was to establish a fund for bail money and defense of clients who were arrested in bar raids.

In spite of the real threat of arrest, the bar remained the social focal point of old gay life. There was simply no other public place where a woman could go to meet other lesbians. The bar in its way was a ghetto, a place in which the stigmatized were hemmed in and allowed to socialize. The old gay bar, as described by women who frequented it, often became the social universe for its clientele, to whom being excluded from it would mean virtual social isolation. Yet, because of the oppressive situation, bar life often emphasized role playing, superficial relationships, and the brooding kind of pessimism or sporadic violence that alcohol can engender.

An "old gay" woman, who experienced the process of liberation and who identifies herself as a political lesbian, talked about her perception of bars and their function:

> Before I developed politically I was satisfied to just play pool and drink, I *figured that's all a lesbian does* [my stress]. But now I'm breaking away from that, it's hard for me to go back to the bars. . . . I don't want to give it the cliché that I'm down on the bar crowd. I'm not. Like, there's a time and need for—even *I* go to the bars. . . .

Q: For what?

A: To escape a lot of times. But if you're looking for something more, it's hard to get it. I was looking for something more. Than escape. Than alcohol. Than drugs. Than, you know—

Q: Well, isn't a bar a place where people meet other people? And sometimes get into a relationship?

A: I have *never* met someone with whom I got in a—even *considered* a relationship with that I met in a bar if that's all there is to their dimension. Unless they had other things. But those were never revealed or came into focus in the bar.

I have good friends that hang around bars—strictly a bar crowd. But even now, because of my political consciousness, I'm kind of growing away from them. But when I want just escape, just to relax, kid around, jive and whatever—I go to the bars. I like to play pool sometimes to get away from the other games in the bars. . . . Ever since I can put bars in proper perspective, I've been able to—I don't leave as frustrated because I know that's all I'm going to have. You can't expect any more than escapism.

Bars fill a gap in me when there is a gap. I get lonely a lot of times, and a lot of times there is no rap or women's movement rap to go to and I just want to be with gay people. You can't be out in the streets and meet with gay people. Sometimes I use the bars to help deal with pain. Sometimes I need to drink. And I'm not an alcoholic or a drinker. But sometimes I *need* to take that edge off— because you know you're not always going to be feeling this way. And just giving it time—

Finally, to summarize some of the aspects of old gay life often mentioned by informants who remember it as an unrelievedly depressing and sometimes destructive experience, a prominent lesbian-feminist described what a recent visit to her hometown lesbian bar elicited in her:

What it meant to go back was to tell dirty jokes, sexist jokes that put down women, that put down lesbians, that rarely put down straight men. It meant playing all kinds of

eye games, making all kinds of innuendos and double en-
tendres, like who is looking at whom, when, and what that
means. "Do you really want to go to bed with me and what
will your lover say if that's true?" And attempting to
somehow measure out what the jealousies are and to what
extent they would be carried. I went through a terrible
ten-year period of destructive emotions in my relationships
because we were into those possessive patterns.

I think now that those patterns were, for me, sick, and
that's not to say that all lesbians in the closet behave that
way—it's just that's what I and some of my friends were
forced to, given the realities of the outside world. So we
spent a lot of time hiding, and that made those experiences, which were bad enough in themselves, much more
intense . . . somehow there was this cloak that had to be
cast over everything we did [angrily] and that's what's so
heavy, because you can't even be angry without somebody
thinking "Aha, that's an unnatural relationship!" And
clearly, that's what does it to you and what makes you sick
is that fact that it's, you know, "unnatural." And that's
what makes all this violence is the "unnaturalness" in their
relationships. . . .

When I say I was back into possessiveness and so on, I
mean back into thinking of other women as objects and
back into wanting to play the kinds of games that mess up
the monogamous relationship—bedswapping, and titillat-
ing ourselves with that kind of threat of violence—"What
will so and so do if she finds out"—and suicide threats and
all the rest of it that has been at some point in my life part
of who I was. . . .

These sentiments reflect the despair of the stigmatized when
they feel that life has little meaning and that there are no viable
alternatives for them.

Homophile Organizations: The Daughters of Bilitis

It was the founding of the lesbian organization the Daughters
of Bilitis, in San Francisco in 1955, that ushered in a new era of
lesbian conciousness and ultimately helped to pave the way for
the more militant and far-reaching demands of the liberation

movements in the following decade. The differences between
the two kinds of organizations have been described by Roxanna
Sweet (1968) and Dennis Altman (1971). Sweet designates the
first homophile organizations, including the Daughters of Bilitis,
as "norm-oriented" in that "they are reacting to already existing
norms within the context of a value system in which they themselves believe." Contrasted with this designation, I believe, are
the "value-oriented" liberation movement groups in which "a
basic reconstitution of self and society and of the relationships
between members of society are demanded" (Sweet, pp. 183–
184).

Dennis Altman describes in more detail the differences between the "civil rights liberalism" of the earlier groups, including the Daughters of Bilitis, and the liberation groups:

> No longer is the claim made that gay people can fit into
> American society, that they are as decent, as patriotic, as
> clean-living as anyone else. Rather, it is argued, it is Amer-
> ican society itself that needs to change. . . .
> The earliest groups tended to act as mutual-support
> groups for homosexuals who half-believed the stereotypes
> about themselves; during the sixties, there was develop-
> ment toward more open demands, even confrontation of
> and protest against social discrimination. But gay libera-
> tion represents a new self-affirmation and determination
> that if anyone will be "cured," it is those who oppress
> rather than those oppressed. . . .
> What the liberation movements call for is a "total
> transformation of society." (p. 119)

Social change sometimes takes place for individuals when
existing limits that function to keep members of a group oppressed are no longer defined as binding and new alternatives
are developed. Martin and Lyon described the social climate felt
by lesbians in the 1950s.

> Most Lesbians were completely downtrodden, having
> been brainwashed by a powerful heterosexual church and
> by the much touted precepts of psychoanalysts. . . . Les-
> bians were isolated, and separated—and scared. (p. 224)

There was good reason for this fear; it was a time when, during the McCarthy period, hundreds of employees of the federal government had been arbitrarily fired, many just on the suspicion of being homosexuals, while locally, raids on lesbian bars had been stepped up as a form of harassment by the police. It is significant that it was during such a period of repression of homosexuals in America that the idea for the organization of a social club for lesbians came from a woman who had been raised in another culture and who, therefore, was not as intimidated by the limitations on lesbians as were her American friends.

Still, the need for secrecy was apparent. When the eight founders of the group, including Del Martin and Phyllis Lyon, first met in a private home, they chose the name Daughters of Bilitis from the poem "Songs of Bilitis," written by Pierre Louys in 1894 about a young student of Sappho's at Lesbos. Excerpts from this lyric love poem include the lines:

> Formerly I was amorous of the beauty of young men, and the remembrance of their words kept me awake.... Today and forever, Mnasidika possesses me. What she receives as a sacrifice is the happiness of those whom I have deserted for her. (Louys, 1951, p. 232)

It was felt by the founders that Daughters of Bilitis was an appropriate name for two reasons: it alluded to a poem in which lesbian love was depicted in a romantic manner, and it was thought to be esoteric enough so that the reference would be apparent only to, in Goffman's terms, "the wise" (1963, p. 28), while to others it would seem to be a name similar to Daughters of the American Revolution, of the Golden West, and the like.

Members were recruited from friends and acquaintances of the founders. Attendance at meetings during the first year ranged from four to sixteen. The meetings were held in the homes of the members, and from the beginning the anonymity of members was carefully protected. The group held three functions monthly: a business meeting, a social, and a discussion session in which the problems the members faced as lesbians were discussed. As the discussions continued, it became obvious to some of the members that there was a need (1) for broader education about lesbianism both for the lesbian herself and for members of the larger culture, (2) for legal reform concerning laws and the negative attitudes about homosexuality perpetrated by the traditional institutions including the church, and (3) for unbiased research on the nature of homosexuality.

However, the need to broaden the function of the organization was evident to only some of the members. It was later realized that the subsequent split between those members who wanted to broaden the purpose of the group and those who preferred to maintain a secret social club was based on class differences. The working-class members wanted a social club, while the middle-class members, who had some experience with the direction they proposed for the club, wanted to work for change in the attitudes toward lesbianism. (Martin and Lyon, p. 222) There was so much conflict that some of the members split off and formed two secret lesbian social clubs, Quatrefoil and Hale Aikane. Both groups are now defunct.

The eight founders of the Daughters of Bilitis were unaware at first that there were other, male-oriented, homophile organizations in existence. Though there is documentation of homosexual organizations in America as early as the late 1800s (Sweet, p. 108), it was not until 1950, with the founding of the Mattachine Society for male homosexuals in Los Angeles, that the first homophile organization dedicated to the premise "that homosexual populations constitute a minority group subject to legal and social discriminations similar to those faced by other minority groups" was founded (Sweet, p. 110). It was the concept that homosexuals were a *minority group* rather than individual "deviants" that represented a new step in the development of group consciousness. It meant that homosexuals could join together and follow the examples of other such groups—most prominently the Negro civil rights movement—to plan programs to promote a change of attitude toward the group by exemplary behavior, through education and research. Subsequently, there emerged male-organized homophile groups that were less moderate. The Society for Individual Rights, incorporated in 1963, is the largest and best known of these.

In the early days of the Daughters of Bilitis, the Mattachine Society was helpful to the fledgling organization. The contact with Mattachine also extended the contacts of the Daughters of Bilitis with members of other homophile organizations and helped to familiarize them with the problems common to the homophile movement as a whole. The male groups were open to homosexuals of both sexes; the Daughters of Bilitis, however, restricted their membership to women. There were often co-alititons of male homosexuals and lesbians over the years, but in the experience of the women involved, the men tended to dominate the groups, while the women often served to inject a voice of temperance.

The main focus of the Daughters of Bilitis members was on their own organization and on helping to alleviate the plight of the lesbian, whose problems and interests differed from those of homosexual men. Since the homophile movement in San Francisco was small, communication between the various organizations was easy to maintain.

The purpose of the Daughters of Bilitis was to engender self-acceptance and society's acceptance of the lesbian: through education, including discussion groups, public forums, and a speaker's bureau; by providing social functions in which she could expand her social networks; through participation in responsible research about homosexuality; and in legal reform to protect the rights of homosexuals (original statement of purpose, reprinted July 25, 1973, on a flyer).

Thus, by offering a range of activities, the members could choose the degree to which they became involved: for those interested only in socializing, there were monthly get-togethers and the discussion groups; for those more interested in educational projects, there were the speaker's bureau, the public forums, and a newsletter to put out; all of these activities functioned to legitimize the lesbian.

Another dimension was added to the early lesbian movement with the publication by the Daughters of Bilitis in October 1956 of the *Ladder*, a monthly journal, which presented the concepts being raised in the discussion groups and public forums, and included news, reviews, and letters, as well as fiction, poetry, and drawings submitted by its readers. It also periodically included surveys and answers to questionnaires about the subjective experience of lesbianism, to counteract the more widely publicized research being conducted by outsiders.

The response to the publication of the *Ladder* was overwhelming to the small membership of the organization. Apparently there was a real need for such a publication, for mail began pouring in from lesbians who read it and who used the staff to make contact with other lesbians. Throughout its career, an important function of the organization has been to answer this mail and to try to be available to these women by telephone. Many lesbians over the years have come to San Francisco only because they knew about the Daughters of Bilitis from reading the *Ladder*. To many other lesbians who remained isolated, the *Ladder* was their only link with other lesbians and, as such, served as an important outlet for them.

The *Ladder* was not the first lesbian publication in America; a privately printed magazine, *Vice Versa*, had appeared in Los Angeles for nine months in 1947–1948. The *Ladder* was more successful, and continued to be published with increasing circulation from 1956 until 1972, during which time it functioned as a national platform for lesbian issues and concerns.

The Daughters of Bilitis became incorporated as a nonprofit organization in January 1957, and this gave it a sense of permanence and respectability. In the following year, two more chapters were formed, in Los Angeles and in New York City. Subsequent chapters have been formed, re-formed, dissolved, and formed again over the years in several other major cities.

In response to the growing number of chapters, the Daughters of Bilitis sponsored the first national lesbian convention in San Francisco in 1960. With each biennial convention, each in a different city where there were chapters of the organization, publicity for lesbians on a broader scale became possible. Lesbians began to be interviewed by local newspapers and appeared on radio and television shows. With each appearance, the legitimization of lesbians was enhanced to some degree.

As the local chapter of the Daughters of Bilitis became more firmly established, the participation of some of its members in social issues increased. In the early days of the publication of the *Ladder*, information had been published advising lesbians of their rights if arrested, and the organization helped get legal counsel if it was necessary. Later the concerns of the organization shifted to encompass some of the problems that homosexuals in general faced, and members attended and exchanged speakers for various conferences of the homophile movement as a whole. They were active in coalitions with male gay organizations on issues of concern to homosexuals—working, for example, to get a candidate elected who was sympathetic to homosexuals. A major step in ascertaining homosexual rights came when members of Mattachine and the Daughters of Bilitis met with sympathetic legislators to try to get the state sex laws changed, so that acts committed in private between consenting adults would become legal. The politicians pointed out, however, that such activity was premature, unless the church, their major obstacle, supported the new laws.

The homophile organizations had been trying to make contact with the established church for years with little success, since the view of organized religion was that homosexuals were sinners. It was not until 1964, when the Reverend Theodore McIlvenna, a Methodist minister from Glide Memorial Church, helped to found the Council on Religion and the Homosexual, in order to facilitate communication between the established church and the homophile community, that the situation began to change.

The Council was developed after a three-day retreat, which consisted of ten members of the male homophile community, five members of the Daughters of Bilitis, and fifteen members of the clergy from throughout the country. Roxanna Sweet (1968, p. 119) credits the council for drawing together the homophile groups and facilitating a new direction in their relations with the larger community by legitimizing them.

The catalyst for changing the subsequent nature of the interaction between homosexuals and the police was a more dramatic event, however. The now legendary New Year's Ball at California Hall in San Francisco on January 1, 1965, was organized by six homophile organizations, including the Daughters of Bilitis, to raise funds for the newly formed Council on Religion and the Homosexual. Prior to the ball, members of the council had arranged to meet with the police to see that the ball would go smoothly and to be sure that the police were aware that it was a "respectable" event. Yet, on the night of the ball, the police pursued a policy of deliberate harassment by taking photographs of each person entering California Hall, by parking a paddy wagon and several police cars outside the entrance to the building, and by entering the hall themselves. During the evening, three attorneys and a woman council member were arrested for "obstructing an officer in the course of his duties" as they argued with the police at the entry to the hall. In spite of the harassment, more than five hundred homosexuals as well as the heterosexual guests crossed the police line.

The outrage felt by the heterosexuals who had attended the ball, including clergymen and their wives, at this show of harassment led to a politicalization and a strengthening of their commitment to fight for the rights of the homophile community, once they themselves had experienced similar repressive actions at firsthand. This experience ultimately led to a restructuring of relationships between the homophile community and the police, including the establishment of a police liaison from within the Community Relations Unit of the police department; the organization of Citizens' Alert, a twenty-four-hour-a-day "hotline" for minority groups in the city as a vehicle against police brutality and harassment; the establishment of the National Sex Forum to educate professionals in various fields about the range of human sexual behavior; and new attention by political groups to the rights of homosexuals. An officer of the police was appointed especially to act as a liaison between the police and the homophile community, homosexual functions were no longer subject to the degree of harassment that had been the practice, and politicians began to attend "candidate nights" sponsored by the homophile organizations for their members. As the homophile community became more aware of its rights and more inclined to educate, agitate, and fight for them, the awareness of a homosexual voting bloc initially estimated at 120,000 (presently estimated at 200,000), led politicians to take the demands of the community more seriously.

The Daughters of Bilitis continued to thrive, its focus still on encouraging acceptance of the lesbian. Though it tried hard to recruit members who cut across class and race lines, it remained largely a middle-class, white organization. Because of state laws against contributing to the delinquency of minors, women under the legal age, though often badly in need of such an organization, could not become members. One underage lesbian tried to form a group for underage lesbians, but it did not last long.

By the late sixties the average member of the Daughters of Bilitis was in her middle twenties. At the weekly discussion meetings, older women, many of them early members, felt somewhat out of place. They, too, formed a social group, Slightly Older Lesbians, that meets once a month at the home of one of the members—one is supposed to be thirty or older to attend. There is presently a more active group, Single Women Over Forty.

Excerpts from field notes give a sense of how a new member views a Daughters of Bilitis meeting. Subjects for discussion are chosen in advance and announced in the monthly calendar in *Sisters* magazine. One typical response to attending a meeting for the first time is "I've never seen so many lesbians in one place before." Another is the expectation that, on entering the room, one may be attacked. (Some women reported that they were amused to find that they were disappointed that this didn't happen). Instead, there is a relaxed feeling to the evening, and no one is pushed to participate if she doesn't feel like doing so. One of my earliest observations from the field notes from November 1972 conveys this point.

> The general feeling was of a pleasant place to be on a rainy night, the women were easy to be with, relaxed. Two couples had their arms around each other; some were touching from time to time, there was none of the militancy I had half expected. Rather, it was a group of about twenty-five women who knew and liked each other or who were there for the first time. There was an atmosphere of letting each woman be herself and a sort of sensible, informed sharing of information and experiences.
>
> One of the officers led the discussion, but very informally. Everyone spoke as it occurred to her to do so, some simply listened, no one interrupted without excusing herself. There were posters on the wall—for example, Be Yourself—as well as lists of such relevant information as legal assistance, health clinic, and crisis-counseling telephone numbers.
>
> The women were mostly in their twenties, many of them were college or graduate students. They did not look different from nonlesbian feminists in their age range. All wore pants, some wore boots, many had long hair, many wore earrings, and some even had on eye makeup—a practice that would have been scorned two years before.
>
> The subject of the conversation was how to reach women who didn't know about the organization but who needed it. The discussion then centered on an earthquake

that was predicted soon for San Francisco. The concern of the group was how to help any woman who might be wounded—they discussed organizing a blood bank and setting up a first aid station for wounded women and children.

The meeting broke up at nine. Everyone was invited to go to a nearby womens' bar after the meeting. Those who remained discussed what to include in the next issue of *Sisters* magazine, put out monthly by the local chapter. Everyone who was in the room got an equal vote.

The major theme of the discussion was a concern for women in general and the desire to help them. The discussions serve to provide information or support for lesbians, based on the experiences of other women who have had similar experiences. So widespread is the sense that the Daughters of Bilitis is a good place to make contact with the general lesbian community that one heterosexual mother even brought her eighteen-year-old lesbian daughter there as the best way to introduce her into the lesbian community.

While two founders of the organization, Del Martin and Phyllis Lyon, went on to work actively for other political causes, the function of the group remained less politically oriented and more concerned with education and with serving as the vehicle for coming out for the many women who needed such an organization. The membership included a core group that ran the organization, worked hard to arrange the weekly meetings, put out the monthly journal, and maintained the large correspondence with lesbians from all over the country. A larger group of members attended periodic meetings and helped with the activities and included—perhaps characteristic of this kind of organization—women who were new in town, who came to the meetings as their first contact with the lesbian community, who soon met other women with similar interests, or met a woman who became a lover and then dropped out of the organization, tying into other social networks.

At the time of the field research, the local chapter of the Daughters of Bilitis was thriving, and many of the core members were feminists who felt that their participation in the organization contributed to the general goal of helping women. Yet, as was noted before, by the early seventies, after fifteen years of being the major point of contact for lesbians entering the community, the Daughters of Bilitis was being bypassed by a new group of more political women moving to San Francisco who by then had other options open to them.

Feminism, Gay Liberation, and Lesbian-Feminism

As old gay life represents the first stage in the development of the current lesbian-feminist community, and the homophile, norm-oriented organizations of the 1950s—most characteristically the Daughters of Bilitis—represent an intermediate stage, so the third stage is typified by the activist lesbian-feminist community that now exists. Lesbian-feminism has its roots in and was influenced by other social movements emerging in the late 1960s and early 1970s. These were the sector of the women's movement that tended to be reformist in character: the Women's Liberation Movement, which was more activist; the Gay Liberation Front, whose roots were in the hippie movement but which borrowed some of the techniques developed in women's liberation. From those developed what was ultimately loosely described as lesbian-feminism, in that it identified with the principles and goals of feminism but had a lesbian focus. The model for these social movements was the Black Power movement, which emerged in the middle 1960s and which was characterized by both separatism from forces of oppression, and activism toward basic social change.

The Women's Movement and Women's Liberation

The current women's movement has its roots in the Women's Rights Movement of the last century, when women banded together to agitate for the right to vote. Once that right was granted, the movement disbanded and the position of women began to deteriorate. Women, though exercising their right to vote, did not identify as a group with other women, rather they tended to be defined by their husband's or father's status.

During World War II many women developed a sense of professional competence when they were pressed into service to replace the men who were at war, at both professional and blue-collar levels. In the late 1940s and early 1950s, after the men had returned to take up their jobs, women seemed to accept the view of themselves as homemakers or instigators of "togetherness," a phrase used in the media to refer to harmonious family life. Many women felt that they were forced into the roles of homemaker and mother and that there were no alternatives. They wondered why they felt so often dissatisfied.

In the 1950s and 1960s, two books written by women were published which helped to articulate the plight of middle-class women and which had great influence in the subsequent development of the women's movement. The earlier was *The Second Sex*, by Simone de Beauvoir, whose central thesis was that since patriarchal times women have been forced to occupy a secondary place in the world in relation to men; this secondary status is not biologically determined, rather, it is due to men's social and educational repression of women. The second book was Betty Friedan's *The Feminine Mystique*, which articulated the psychic morass in which many contemporary middle-class housewives found themselves. It was partly the overwhelming reaction by middle-class women to Friedan's book, which helped define the problem many women were having, plus the lack of enforcement of the sex provision in the Equal Pay Act in 1964 (which demonstrated once again that women as a group were not taken seriously), that led to the formation of the National Organization for Women (NOW) in 1966. NOW has been described as "the first militant feminist group in the twentieth century to combat sex discrimination in all spheres of life: social, political, economic, psychological" (Hole and Levine, 1971, p. 82). Because a large percentage of NOW's original members were middle-class and professional women, NOW tended to work for reform within the establishment, a position that appealed to conservative and moderate feminists.

Because of NOW's reformist position, women who held more radical views about the nature of social change either split off from NOW to form their own groups or developed new energies in already existing groups of radical feminists, many of whom had developed the basis for feminist separatist politics within women's caucuses in the student, peace, and civil rights movements. A distinction between the two groups is that the women's rights movement, as exemplified by NOW, focuses on external reform of social institutions, while women's liberation, which developed from a more radical base, emphasizes the internal raising of consciousness as a basis for action. Both branches of the feminist movement work toward the same goal, elimination of the sex-role system (Hole and Levine, p. 398).

The development of NOW, the reformist branch of the women's movement, remained highly structured and fairly well organized, while the liberation branch, though developing important techniques and theoretical analyses, was more amorphous. According to Sally Gearhart, most of the activist lesbian-feminists in the San Francisco community came to their political commitment through the liberation sector of the women's movement.

There is a further distinction. From the beginning of the first meetings of groups of women in what was to be the liberation sector of the movement, there were two factions, each with differing priorities. Hole and Levine refer to them as "politicos" and "feminists" and describe the differences:

> As the movement grew it became more and more clear that at the core of the dispute was a profound disagreement about the source of women's subjugation. Politicos accept for the most part the Marx-Engels critique of society which locates the source of oppression in the family, the first institution of private property and the division of labor, and by extension, capitalism. Feminists, on the other hand, although most of them are also critical of capitalism, argue that the male-defined social institutions and value structure, both of which stereotype people on the basis of sex roles, are responsible for women's status. (p. 109).

Apart from these two groups in women's liberation, there is a large group of women who affiliate with the small groups that form the structure of women's liberation, who feel the need to belong to such groups but who have no well-articulated political orientation.

As women's liberation developed, it made important theoretical and tactical contributions to the women's movement as a whole. Various groups have been credited with specific contributions.

Women's liberation began in Chicago and New York with radical women from the New Left who had attended the National Conference for a New Politics in Chicago in 1967, a year after the founding of NOW. They had asked to have a resolution of women's issues presented, but instead were patronized by men of the New Left, who refused. Enraged by this treatment, the women began meeting regularly to analyze the nature of women's roles in leftist politics.

Shulamith Firestone, who later wrote *The Dialectic of Sex* (1970), and Pamela Allen, who wrote *Free Space: A Perspective on the Small Group in Women's Liberation* (1970), organized New York City's first women's group, Radical Women. The members, in keeping with their political orientation, wanted to take action, and they planned a demonstration during an antiwar protest. Their rationale was that women must begin to deal with their own oppression or they will continue to be powerless. The demonstration was the first public action undertaken by radical women to engage the attention of other women. During their protest the slogan "Sisterhood is Powerful" was used for the first time.

By 1968, women's groups throughout the country began to form; in San Francisco, for example, the first small women's group, Sudsofloppen, was formed in 1968. The group developed into a vehicle that changed the lives of the women involved and forged a political entity among the group members, which became a prototype of a small group committed to radical action through a consciousness-raising process of talking about their feelings, sharing the experiences, analyzing the situation, and abstracting from it for further action (Allen, pp. 49-50).

This process was developed during the meetings of the New York Radical Women, and it enabled women to see their isolated personal experiences as the results of a social cause which had a political solution (Sarachild, 1975, p. 132). From the experiences in these sessions came the slogan "the personal is political." The individual groups were to become the cell of a mass liberation movement; the content of the group discussions depended on the backgrounds of its members, while the consciousness-raising experience itself served as a catalyst toward politicization (Hole and Levine, p. 137).

The widespread use of consciousness-raising as an organizing and educational tool is credited to Redstockings, a New York-based militant feminist organization, which saw such groups as a "structured way of overcoming the individual 'ghettoization' of women from one another." It emphasized that women are a class, that individual relationships between women and men are in reality class relationships, and that the conflicts between them are political conflicts that can only be solved collectively (p. 137). Women in the movement make the distinction that consciousness-raising is not therapy, that "the purpose of therapy is individual change in behavior, that the purpose of consciousness-raising is collective programs for liberation based on the concrete realities of our lives" (p. 138).

The concept of egalitarianism was added to feminist theory and practice when Ti-Grace Atkinson resigned as president of the New York chapter of NOW because she disagreed with its hierarchical structure. She helped to form a theory-action group, the Feminists, who stressed egalitarianism among its members. This practice led to unstructured sessions without leaders, a technique intended to break down arbitrary distinctions among women, such as education and class membership. Egalitarianism has become a basic part of feminist practice; more recently, however, some women have begun to structure certain activities so as to share knowledge and to give them more stability.

Lesbians and the Women's Movement

Some of the earliest members of the women's movement were women who were lesbians; however, they felt that they had to keep silent about their affectional preference and chose to iden-tify with other women as feminists, since they feared ostracism if their lesbian identity were known. Many lesbians were drawn to the women's movement; since they were not dependent on men for either emotional gratification or financial support, they had an interest in working for equal job opportunities for women, and they were not torn apart, as other feminists might be, by a commitment to feminism while living with a man.

During the early days of NOW lesbian members were thought to be a hindrance to the movement by officers who felt that to make an issue of lesbianism would detract from the purpose of the organization, which was to fight sexism (Abbott and Love, 1972, p. 134). Outspoken lesbians in NOW pointed out that women who felt that way were guilty of sexism themselves in discriminating against other women because of their sexual preference as lesbians. By its rejection of lesbians, NOW triggered another split, which led to the formation of groups of gay feminists who, as the Radicalesbians, wrote a classic position paper, "The Woman-Identified Woman," for the 1970 Congress to Unite Women, a large coalition of women's groups. They also planned action to force discussion on the issue of lesbianism and feminism.

Excerpts from the paper, which has been widely quoted and which articulates some of the basic assumptions of lesbian-feminism, follow.

What is a lesbian? A lesbian is the rage of all women condensed to the point of explosion. She is the woman who, often beginning at an extremely early age, acts in accordance with her inner compulsion to be a more complete and freer human being than her society... cares to allow her.... At some level she has not been able to accept the limitations and oppression laid on her by the most basic role of her society—the female role....

Lesbianism, like male homosexuality, is a category of behavior possible only in a sexist society characterized by rigid sex roles and dominated by male supremacy. Those sex roles dehumanize women by defining us as a supportive/serving caste in relation to the master caste of men, and emotionally cripple men by demanding that they be alienated from their own bodies and emotions in order to perform their economic/political/military functions effectively....

The investment in keeping women in that contemptuous role is very great. Lesbian is the word, the label, the condition that holds women in line.... Lesbian is a label invented by the man to throw at any woman who dares to be his equal, who dares to challenge his prerogatives... who dares to assert the primacy of her own needs... a lesbian is not considered a "real woman." And yet, in popular thinking, there is really only one essential difference between a lesbian and other women—*the essence of being a "woman" is to get fucked by men* (my stress).... Are we going to continue the male classification system of defining all females in sexual relations to some other category of people? Affixing the label lesbian not only to a woman who aspires to be a person, but also to any situation of real love, real solidarity, real primacy among women is a primary form of divisiveness among women; it is the condition which keeps women within the confines of the feminine role, and it is the debunking/scare term that keeps women from forming any primary attachments, groups, or associations among ourselves. . . .

As the source of self-hate and the lack of real self are rooted in our male-given identity, we must *create a new sense of self—that identity we have to develop with reference to ourselves and not in relation to men. This consciousness is the revolutionary force from which all else will follow* (my stress). . . . For this we must be available and supportive to one another. . . . Our energies must flow toward our sisters, not backwards toward our oppressors. . . .

It is the primacy of women relating to women, of women creating a new consciousness of and with each other which is at the heart of women's liberation, and the basis for the cultural revolution. . . . With that real self, with that consciousness, we begin a revolution to end the imposition of all coercive identifications, and to achieve maximum autonomy in human expression.

At the conference, many lesbians wore T-shirts identifying themselves as the Lavender Menace and charged the women's movement with discrimination against their lesbian sisters. Other women—some lesbian and some not—joined them in a show of solidarity. The following day workshops were held on lesbian issues, and an all-women's dance was held attended by both lesbians and heterosexual women (Abbott and Love, p. 114). Further contact between women's liberation members and lesbians, many belonging to the Gay Liberation Front, took place.

Some of those in power at NOW, afraid of a "lesbian takeover," saw to it that officers and programs favorable to lesbians were phased out. By 1970 there was a swing among many of those in power in NOW against the lesbian issue. Abbott and Love describe in detail the factors leading to this and to NOW's subsequent acceptance in detail of lesbianism as a legitimate cause in the liberation of all women (pp. 107–134). By then many lesbians had become impatient with NOW and had either joined the Gay Liberation Front or become members of mixed or all-lesbian small groups under the aegis of women's liberation.

Gay Liberation

Meanwhile, as the model of liberation groups of oppressed minorities appeared to be effective in changing the participants' sense of themselves as isolated and helpless, while apparently causing some social change, homosexuals also banded together in a gay liberation group. Though there were beginning to be militant gay organizations based on the models of women's liberation groups before June 1969, it was the Stonewall riots that took place at that time in New York City which crystallized a new image of Gay and Proud, Gay and Activist.

The Stonewall Inn was a homosexual dance bar off Sheridan Square in Greenwich Village. The police raided the bar over alleged infringement of the liquor laws, a not uncommon occurrence. What made the difference was that the gays, for the first time, fought back in a united action, which lasted for three days and brought support from people all over the area. The exhilaration felt by those who took part in the action was analogous to the experience of student activists; it helped to forge a sense of community and of new political possibilities, which led to the formation of the Gay Liberation Front, named after the National Liberation Front in Vietnam (Altman, pp. 117–118). The Stonewall riots are commemorated every year with Gay Power parades in several cities with large gay populations. In 1977 it was estimated that about 200,000 women and men took part in the Gay Pride parade in San Francisco.

The Stonewall riots and the founding of the Gay Liberation Front in New York were crucial elements in the radical politicalization of many gays; however, the gay liberation movement as a whole was always more heavily made up of men than of lesbians, who at that time were more likely to affiliate with feminist groups. Based on the women's liberation groups, gay liberation consciousness-raising groups had sprung up independently in California and New York a few months before the

Stonewall riots (Altman, p. 116). In San Francisco, some direct action against institutions oppressive to gays had already been taken, particularly protests and picketing.

Meanwhile, even among the more traditional homophile groups, the impact of feminism was felt when lesbians who had been working with male homosexuals realized that many of them were as sexist as heterosexual men. The turning point in San Francisco came at the male-dominated North American Conference of Homophile Organizations (NACHO) in 1972 when representatives from lesbian organizations accused the men of sexism and called for separation. Del Martin later wrote a position paper entitled "If That's All There Is" calling for separation from gay men and consolidation with other lesbians.

By 1970 in the Bay Area, there began to be a split as well between lesbians and heterosexual women in the women's liberation small groups. The dynamics of the small-group situation was such that many lesbians had first come out in their mixed groups, where they found support but also realized that they had more in common with their lesbian sisters than with most heterosexual feminists. Soon they were separating into their own all-lesbian groups whose purpose was to develop a specifically lesbian-feminist awareness.

Women's Gay Liberation Groups

The organization of small groups in the Bay Area spread. In 1970 there were an estimated sixty-four women's small groups. Since the individual groups were seen by some theorists as cells for a mass movement, representatives of the groups met at Glide Memorial Church for a general meeting once a month. Many of the early groups became more political in orientation and became collectives, working for some specific project in the women's community, such as the Women's Training Center (see chapter four). Others became political study groups, progressing from consciousness-raising to a more structured political analysis. Since then, new groups continually have been organized and then have spun off. Most of the women in the community have been part of the small-group process as part of their introduction into a lesbian-activist community.

It is the small-group process which most characteristically serves as a reorientation for feminists and for the political lesbian. From the gay liberation movement came the concept of gay pride; from the women's liberation movement came the sense that the oppression of women and of lesbians was political and that the first step was to join a support group made up of women with similar experiences, so that both direction for action and a new sense of bonding with other women could take place.

Esther Newton and Shirley Walton suggest, in "The Person Is Political," that women who become committed feminists through the consciousness-raising process "experience deep, pervasive changes in their world view, personal relationships, personalities, jobs, goals" (p. 43). They see this process as analogous to a conversion experience, and have found that the most important factors in sustaining a conversion were support and segregation. The group functions to "change a woman's identity and cognition to a new reality and ...support ...the woman during that change ...[then] the women begin to look for more specific and active means of living their new perceptions within the movement" (p. 50).

As lesbians began to separate from both gay men and heterosexual women a rather curious phenomenon took place. Many heterosexual feminists began to define lesbians as "the vanguard of the movement"—the purest form of feminism—since lesbians did not cohabit with the enemy and already had to be self-sufficient and self-defining women. While it is true that many young women who came out within the context of the movement would have been lesbians anyway, the practice of some heterosexually oriented women to identify themselves as lesbian as a political gesture of solidarity seemed somewhat oppressive and superficial to lesbians who had come out before the movement and had suffered real oppression.

Some lesbians also resented heterosexual feminists who would use the emotional energy of their lesbian sisters for support in small groups and then go back to their men, or would want to have a physical relationship with a lesbian as part of a "social experiment" and perhaps cause suffering to the lesbian who fell in love with her. Part of the motivation for lesbian separatism was the need for lesbians to develop support groups based on their own specific needs.

As lesbians became feminists, experienced the small-group

situations, and then split off to evolve theories specific to their situation and experience, what might loosely be defined as lesbian-separatism coalesced. Eisenstein talks about it in "Connections Between Class and Sex":

> Lesbianism is revolutionary because it challenges the basic organization of the family, the sexual division of labor, and the heterosexual world.
>
> The lesbian alternative challenges those dimensions of power which are sexually based. Two of the major positions that have been developed are: (1) that the ultimate goal of feminism is to collapse all sex-role stereotypes such that the normal sexual orientation is bi-sexual and that unless sexual relations with men can be entered on an equal footing, feminists at this time must be lesbians; and (2) that to be a true feminist one must be a lesbian and the only way to avoid oppression by men is to remove all women from contact with men through the creation of self-sufficient communities of lesbians (pp. 15–16).

An essay in *The Furies*, a lesbian-feminist newspaper, further refines these concepts:

> The base of our ideological thought is: Sexism is the root of all other oppression, and Lesbian and women oppression will not end by smashing capitalism, racism, and imperialism. Lesbianism is not a metter of sexual preference, but rather one of political choice which every woman must make if she is to become woman-identified and thereby end male supremacy. Lesbians as outcasts from every culture but their own have the most to gain by ending class, race, and national supremacy within their own ranks. Lesbians must get out of the straight woman's movement and form their own movement in order to be taken seriously, to stop straight women from oppressing us, and to force straight women to deal with their own Lesbianism. Lesbians cannot develop a common politics with women who do not accept Lesbianism as a political issue. (Myron and Bunch, 1975, p. 15)

The concept of lesbianism as a political issue was further developed.

Woman-identified Lesbianism is, then, more than a sexual preference, it is a *political choice* (my stress). It is political because relationships between men and women are essentially political, they involve power and dominance. Since the Lesbian actively rejects that relationship and chooses women, she defies the established political system.... For the Lesbian or heterosexual woman, there is no individual solution to oppression....

Our war against male supremacy does ... involve attacking the latter-day dominations based on class, race and nation. As Lesbians who are outcasts from every group, it would be suicidal to perpetrate these man-made divisions among ourselves.... This does not mean that there is no racism or class chauvinism within us, but we must destroy these divisive remnants of privileged behavior among ourselves as the first step toward their destruction in the society. Race, class, and national oppression come from men, serve ruling-class white men's interests, and have no place in a woman-identified revolution. (pp. 30–31, 33).

By defining lesbianism as *political,* it became a positive and, to some, a revolutionary choice.

Meanwhile, though many women were for the first time identifying themselves as lesbians to mixed groups in the small-group context, it was still difficult to do so publicly. Therefore, when on August 26, 1970, at a large coalition rally in San Francisco sponsored by women's groups to celebrate the anniversary of women's voting rights, a woman on a lesbian panel asked the audience of women how many of them had felt sexual attraction for another woman, it was a significant question. To many lesbians in the audience, to answer this question publicly went against years of self-protection; however, the audience slowly rose, until a quarter, then half, of the audience was standing; than all of the women rose as a gesture of solidarity with their lesbian sisters.

During this period, many activist women who had experienced the small-group process dedicated themselves to developing projects within the context of lesbian-feminism, such as courses in women's studies, self-defense classes, health-care projects, the cohesion of the Women's Centers and Women's

Switchboard, women's coffeehouses, women's printing presses, and aspects of feminist and lesbian culture such as poetry, music, and films, as well as building social networks. Through this process, a lesbian-feminist community developed. We turn now to a more detailed description of that community.

3. THE COMMUNITY

It is impossible to estimate with any degree of accuracy how many lesbians live in San Francisco at any one time, because there is no census in which the designation "lesbian" appears; the lesbian population is somewhat transient; and many women still have reason to hide their affectional orientation. One estimate is that there is a minimum of 35,000 lesbians living in San Francisco, a city whose total population is about 700,000.

The lesbians who live in San Francisco represent a variety of lifestyles and differing degrees of commitment to lesbian life. Some of the women are upper class, often professionals in their fields, who socialize only in their own homes among close friends, and who do not identify themselves with activist lesbianism. Others are women who are closeted; many of these are married to men. Some are women who live quietly with their women partners and do not associate with other lesbians. There are also groups of third-world or working-class lesbians who, if they are active at all in a lesbian political context, confine this activity to their own groups. There is, as well, a large population of women whose only interest and participation in lesbian life centers around the women's bars and their ancillary activities. Finally, there are lesbian-separatists, who define their politics to exclude unnecessary contact with men, with women who are heterosexual, or with lesbians who do not share their political commitment.

This study does not encompass the whole range of local lesbian life. Many women are inaccessible for such a study or feel that to participate would be threatening to them; or their lives are not significantly different from what they were before the liberation movements. Since this work focuses on the mutual influence of lesbianism and feminism, the population herein described consists of the large number of women who, because of their world view and activities, choose to identify themselves as lesbian-feminists, in that they adhere to the precepts of feminism, as was described in chapter two. Because their social identity as lesbians is an organizing principle in their lives, their energies are directed first toward their own community of kind and its special needs, rather than toward the betterment of the lot of women in general. Their political orientation might be described as ranging between two positions of lesbian-feminism: lesbian cultural feminism and lesbian feminist socialism, with many women embracing a combination of the two. By this I mean that, as feminists, they want equality for women and a breakdown of sex-role stereotyping, yet they emphasize the values of self-reliance within the context of a strong support group. As cultural feminists, they have rediscovered and revivified the symbols of women's strength and the spiritual aspects of the feminine principle. As socialists, they are working toward the breakdown of capitalism, racism, imperialism, oppressive practices toward the disadvantaged, and the effects of a capitalist culture on the disadvantaged, and also the effects of a capitalist culture on those raised in it.

The methods they use to reach these goals vary. The techniques used by the politically oriented to accomplish their stated goals are small problem-solving and study groups, in which self-criticism sessions are held in order to help the individual work toward a collective group identity and politically directed actions. Women who are more interested in spiritual development are constructing rituals based on female symbols, developing healing powers and intuition between group members, reconstructing a more female-oriented history than now exists, and using traditional occult methods such as tarot and white witchcraft to focus on life-generating forces.

The lesbian community in San Francisco is not a traditional community in the sense that it has geographical boundaries; rather it is

A continuing collectivity of individuals who share some significant activity and who out of a history of continuing interaction based on that activity begin to generate a sense of bounded group possessing special norms and a particular argot.... Various kinds of social activity reinforce a feeling of identity and provide for the homosexual a way of institutionalizing the experience, wisdom, and mythology of the collectivity. (Simon and Gagnon, 1967b, p. 261)

There is a precedence in referring to the homosexual collectivity as a community. Evelyn Hooker, in her pioneer study of the male homosexual group in Los Angeles, suggested:

If one is permitted to use the term [community] to refer to an aggregate of persons engaging in common activities, sharing common interests, and having a feeling of sociopsychological unity with variations in the degree to which persons have these characteristics ...then it is completely germane to homosexuals. (1961, p. 43)

Elizabeth Barnhart, in describing a lesbian counterculture community in Oregon (1975), points out that

the primary function of the community is to provide the members with a psychological kin group. Secondary to this main function, and because of it, the individual is able to achieve economic stability, to be instructed on behavior and values of community membership, and to form pair relationships.... A feeling of *esprit de corps* appears to give the members a feeling of security, identity, and ego enhancement.

The terms "community," "lesbian community," and "women's community" are commonly used by the women themselves to refer to the continuing social networks of lesbians who are committed to the lesbian-feminist lifestyle, who participate in various community activities and projects, and who congregate socially. The concept "socio-psychological unity" is to them an important part of their sense of what a community is and who belongs to it.

The Community

San Francisco As a Center for Homosexual Life

Though there is a large turnover, it has been estimated that by 1977 about 200,000 homosexual women and men, out of a total population of 715,000, live in San Francisco at any one time. To many homosexuals of both sexes, San Francisco is recognized both nationally and internationally as a tolerant city and a center for gay culture.

> San Francisco ... has become a haven for homosexuals from all over the nation. ... This city has become an oasis in a desert of extensive legal and social abuse that permeates many other communities. (*Datebook, San Francisco Chronicle*, November 7, 1976)

There are historical precedents for San Francisco as a more liberal city in its tolerance of a wide range of behavior than many other American cities. One reason is that San Francisco, like New Orleans, was settled by people with a Mediterranean Catholic heritage—unlike the more conservative New England towns, which were settled by English Protestants—who brought to San Francisco a more laissez-faire approach to the behavior of others. Then, too, from its earliest days, San Francisco was a seaport, in which people from many cultures mixed easily. During the gold rush, with a sudden influx of people from all over the world and a lack of organized social restraints, the city "burst through conventional social controls" (Becker, 1971, p.9). From that time, the concept of San Francisco as a glamorous and wicked place became part of the city's lore, and may persist even today for both newcomers and city residents.

San Francisco has also traditionally been a center for Bohemians—artists and writers who congregated in the North Beach and Russian Hill areas. More recently, in the late 1950s, San Francisco came to the attention of the nation as the home of the Beat Generation. In the following decade, with the introduction of hallucinogenic drugs, the counterculture flourished as the attention of the world turned to San Francisco's hippies. Many gays came to San Francisco during the height of the hippie era (1966–1968) because they were attracted to the new lifestyle, and because hippies tended to be nonjudgmental about homosexuality.

Aside from its history as a sophisticated city that tolerates a variety of lifestyles, there is another reason why San Franciscans, as a whole, are less concerned about a large population of homosexuals than most citizens of other cities. For a city of its size, San Francisco has an unusually large single and childless population.[1] This demographic factor reduces the number of those parents who, fearing for the welfare of their children, might put pressure on politicians who tolerate a homosexual community in their midst.

As homosexuals became aware of the political implications of their numbers, they organized a potential voting bloc of a now estimated 200,000 people. As local political candidates became aware of the impact of the homosexual vote (largely male), many of them began to court it. The effects of this had concrete advantages for the homosexual community, most prominently in April 1972 when a clause was added to the city code stating that the city will not do business with any firm that discriminates by sex or *sexual orientation*. This was the first American civil rights legislation for homosexuals which specifically protects the rights of homosexuals, who cannot be fired if their affectional orientation is discovered. If homosexuals feel that they have been discriminated against, they have recourse, since the city government has hired a gay rights advisor to the Human Rights Commission specifically to investigate their complaints. By 1976, three homosexuals, two women and one man, had been appointed by the mayor to city commissions. Though there is still some discrimination against homosexuals in San Francisco, the fact that the city government has taken official steps to protect their rights and to represent them, substantiates their belief that San Francisco is a "gay mecca." In fact, San Francisco is probably the only city in America in which members of the police department officially hold an annual softball game with a team representing the gay community.

Homosexuals have been drawn to San Francisco not only because of its reputation as a tolerant place to live, in which

1. Out of a total population of 592,287 women and men living in the city of San Francisco, 398,061 are single, according to the 1970 United States Census. Of 164,436 families, 94,766 do not have children living with them. (Both figures were given to me by Lee Smith of the Documents Room of the San Francisco Public Library.)

their rights are protected. There are other reasons related to the nature of the existing homosexual community itself. For lesbians, there were several attractions in San Francisco. There was the lesbian organization, the Daughters of Bilitis, and the publicity it received through its journal, the *Ladder*, which let lesbians know that there were others "like themselves" in San Francisco; the widespread attention to the publication of *Lesbian/Woman* (Martin and Lyon, 1972) brought publicity to the local community; and finally, as a visible lesbian-feminism emerged, many women already committed to lesbian activism, hearing about it or meeting its members at lesbian conventions, came to San Francisco to join a group already defined as both political and supportive.

Women who come to San Francisco to become part of the community are likely to make contact through entry points like the Women's Switchboard, by hanging around the women's coffeehouses or bars, through courses in women's studies, through projects, or through personal contacts. One woman describes, in a taped interview, how she and her partner got in touch with the community.

> When I first came out here on vacation, I had the name of a friend from New York. Then when my lover and I decided to come out here and live, I looked her up. She was living in a house with a lot of other lesbians, so we started spending time with them. Through them we met other women, two of whom lived with us for awhile. Then I began working on a women's conference on health and the lesbians had a separate meeting and later got together in a study group. I met a lot of my friends through that. Then that fall, I went back to school and met some more women, and two of them moved close by. So being in activities, and functions, and working for the community, at parties, at people's houses—you get to know who's who and really feel part of a group. It's friends and friends of friends. But it's also when you're doing more stuff is when you meet people.

Apart from qualities that the local lesbian community shares with similar communities in other large cities, there are particular characteristics that are often mentioned both by women who have come to live in San Francisco and by visitors. One of these is that, though a basic value of lesbian-feminism everywhere is support for one's sisters, the San Francisco community is felt to be an especially supportive group. As one woman who has lived in several cities with sizable lesbian population says:

All the women [here] are not active, say active going to meetings, but those women are there when you need them! That support that Bay Area women—because I'm sure that it isn't the same elsewhere—it's like women *specifically* [laughs] came here to support other women! Those women who are really into women are *here*. They're not in L.A. They come up here from L.A. It's really strange, because that's women from all over the whole country who come here to be a part of the Gay Women's Movement. It's really fine. Keep those ladies coming.

The local community is part of a network of other such communities across the country. Communication among them is through visitors, telephone calls, and letters. Women who come from other parts of the country expect to be put up by friends or friends of friends who live here. Through these contacts, local women learn what is happening both with friends in other communities and nationally. While women who come to visit often decide to stay and add to the community store of knowledge, there are other forms of communication. Many newspapers, magazines, and books written by and for lesbian-feminists are available in San Francisco. These transmit news, ideas, and attitudes to their readers and rally them for particular causes. Among the most widely read in San Francisco are *Plexus*, a monthly feminist newspaper published in the East Bay, which has a calendar of local events of interest to women; the San Francisco Women's Centers and Switchboard monthly newsletter, which also lists ongoing events; the *Amazon Quarterly* (now defunct) which, though an excellent literary magazine, also served as a forum for ideas; the *Lesbian Tide*, published in Los Angeles, which defines itself as a lesbian-feminist magazine but also solicits articles representing other points of view; and *Sis-*

ters, the monthly magazine put out by the local chapter of the Daughters of Bilitis, which prints art and literature contributed by its readers.

There are also magazines and newspapers from elsewhere that are read locally and are directed to more specific interests. A few examples are *Country Woman*, written for feminists who live in the country, published in Albion, California; *Womanspirit*, stressing spiritual development within a feminist context, from Oregon; and *Quest*, which serves as an analytic and ideological platform, from Washington, D.C.

The point of view of lesbians is also presented on television and local radio. There are periodic panel discussions on local television shows in which lesbians representing different perspectives have appeared. More regular are the two weekly shows on the Berkeley FM radio station, KPFA, on which any member of the lesbian community may submit ideas and make a tape for an hour-long program.

The interchange of ideas is facilitated by conferences and informal gatherings which local women attend. The subjects of interest vary: they may focus on women and music, or the spiritual aspects of lesbianism, or the forging of a new political direction for lesbian-feminism.

Finally, one of the important characteristics of the post-liberation community is the development of and interest in art forms whose content is specifically geared to lesbians. The local community includes songwriters, performers of women's music, artists, writers, and film makers. In out-of-town performances, during women's music weekends, and in the distribution of locally made movies, contributions from San Francisco lesbians are transmitted and become part of the development of a general lesbian culture. At the same time, a continual stream of visitors and the careful attention to media directed to lesbian-feminists, keeps the local community abreast of and contributing to the movement in other parts of the country.

Ingroup Distinctions

A rough estimate of the number of women actively involved in the lesbian-feminist community at any one time is between two and five thousand. Many of these women do not consistently interact with other than members of their own special-

5a/5b. The Berkeley Women's Music Collective making a record. One big change has been the emergence of excellent feminist musicians who are creating a whole new body of music. (Cathy Cade)

interest or friendship groups, but they recognize other community members by sight and are often aware of where they fit into the community structure. When they do interact, it is usually in a specific place. For example, if members of their own group are not present, women may socialize in the two women's coffeehouses, in the seven women's bars and their related activities, at rallies and demonstrations, and at all-women's dances and benefits for community projects. They may be in the same classes in women's studies. In short, they become aware of each other, over time, in contexts defined as part of the community territory or at outside events of interest to community members.

Although active members are aware of which women represent particular factions of the community, they tend to stick with members of their own social and political networks. However, given the surge of history and of personal emotional change, networks as well as the amount and kind of participation in community activities are fluid. A woman who was in a particular social network may, because of a new lover, be incorporated into another network within a short time. She may keep up with individuals from her old group and close friends, but her loyalties will be directed toward the new network as a whole. In other instances, women who have been actively participating in projects over a period of time, may suddenly need to get a full-time job, which precludes such participation, or may just feel "burned out," and simply not participate in any activities at all for awhile. Thus new configurations are constantly developing in the social map of the community.

Since one of the doctrines of lesbian-feminism is the need for an egalitarian community, the community members argue that there is no social structure in the collectivity, since, by its very nature, social structure is based on hierarchical distinctions. In fact, the structure of the community is a series of overlapping social networks, in which friendship groups focus around pair relationships or special interests. Women who are more active in community projects are usually more widely known and may have greater prestige, but there is a concerted effort to do away with "leaders." Within the social networks, women with stronger personalities tend to influence their own groups, but there is a self-conscious effort at maintaining group process in decision making.

The Community

Though one of the community's basic values is mutual support and sisterhood, it would be wrong to give the impression that life in the lesbian community is completely harmonious. As with other special-interest groups, the lesbian community has political factions as well as members who avoid each other for personal reasons. It is perhaps inherent in the nature of a community in which feelings are taken very seriously, and in which the members voluntarily segregate themselves from outsiders, for divisive differences to appear. When this happens, mutual friends may try to mediate, or the women in question may meet to work through the differences between them. If a resolution is not possible, those who are in disagreement may simply agree to disagree. In some cases, this can mean that a woman is no longer part of her original friendship group or pair relationship, and she may then socialize with new sets of people until she is drawn into a new pair relationship or a recognizable social unit.

Within the community, women are identified by their special interests or skills, by their friendship networks, and by their present or former lovers. However, other kinds of distinctions are also made. One is whether a woman came out before or after the liberation movements of the late 1960s—that is, whether she is "old" or "new" gay. If she came out before the movement, it is likely she suffered certain kinds of oppression and had particular experiences within the lesbian social world that contemporary lesbians do not have—most typically contending with the implications of stricter role dichotomes (see p. 43). In some ways, there is a special kind of validity assumed if a woman came out before the movement, in that her impetus to be a lesbian was so strong that she acted on it even in the context of isolation and lack of validation from the culture.

Another distinction made by politically oriented lesbians is whether a woman, "old" or "new" gay, is political. If so, she defines her life within a political framework, most of her activities are directed toward political ends, and her friends are likely to share her interests.

One woman gave a breakdown of what had happened to the lesbians she had known who had participated in the original "consciousness-raising" groups in San Francisco in the late 1960s, who had become feminists through that process (see p. 66). As she explained it in a taped interview, there are roughly four categories. (1) A very few women became isolated from other women and have gone back to trying to live without the support of other women; (2) some women were channeled into a more reformist direction—for example, they are presently active in the local branch of the National Organization of Women, trying to change the system through education and legislation; (3) many women developed an interest in cultural feminism and the spiritual and healing aspects of womanness; (4) other women became very politicized and became oriented toward socialism and third-world-liberation struggles. Some of these women saw class struggle as having a greater priority than lesbian struggle, while others defined the position of lesbians as the focal point of their political commitment.

Spiritual Life

Lesbian-feminists, whether political or cultural, are questioning every aspect of the culture in which they grew up and are redefining within a feminist context even such hallowed concepts as God the Father. Yet, for some women there seems to be a need for spirituality, rituals, and even organized religion.

Most lesbian-feminists are not religious in the traditional sense, since to be so implies the worship of a partiarchal godhead, which contradicts their feminist teachings. Since most traditional religions view homosexuality as a sin, their self-definition as lesbians also precludes participation in organized religion. Instead, alternatives to organized religion have emerged in the community. These include turning to women's spirituality, reinterpretation of traditional religious symbols within a feminist context, or joining a homosexuality-oriented but traditional church.

As a body of knowledge and new practices have been developed by cultural feminists, particularly in the area of women's spirituality, many lesbians have evolved a more personalized awareness of a religious-spiritual identification with their conception of the Mother Goddess. They see the Mother Goddess as the true life force, rudely displaced by the male godhead, whose worship has caused war, pestilence, inhumanity, and the rape of the planet. By getting in touch with the Mother Goddess, they reinforce their strength as women, as part of a history and a future in which both the force and the nurturing elements of women are the foundation. With this in mind, members of the community who worship the Mother Goddess have turned to witchcraft, or have developed rituals that encompass a kind of pantheism and draw strongly on the moon and the earth as symbols of the goddess and the intuition and sisterhood of all women.

Other women retain the cultural symbols of the traditional religions in which they were raised, but they reinterpret them so as to avoid the male godhead and the repression of others. For example, women hold community celebrations in their homes during Easter, Christmas, Chanukah, and Passover, in which they present nonsexist prayers or poems for the occasion. These services function to reinforce the religious identity of the women present, but they do so within the context of their lesbian-feminism.

There is a third possibility for homosexuals who want to worship in a more traditional religious framework: the Metropolitan Community Church, founded by the Reverend Troy Perry, for homosexuals. Not everyone who attends the local branch of the church is a homosexual, though homosexuals are in the majority in the congregation. The services are traditional in form, but they stress brotherhood of mankind and the view of homosexuality as one example of loving one's neighbor. Though there are a few women being trained in the church organization, most lesbian-feminists do not belong to the congregation, because they think it is sexist and that it reinforces patriarchal religious attitudes.

Self-preservation and Personal Characteristics

Women who are members of the lesbian-feminist community were not born into it, they chose to belong. By making that choice, they take on a new social identification and definition of self and therefore look for and welcome external signs that will reinforce their shift in identity. Two of the most significant marks are the public assumption of new names and a change in dress.

The assumption of a new name reflects the desire of the woman to divest herself of every aspect of male domination. Since family names in our culture are derived from the father's line, many women who are feminists, whether or not they are lesbians, change their family names as a symbolic gesture of separation from a male-oriented social identification. Often women take the first name of their own mothers and incorporate it in a new last name. Thus one of the most articulate members of the early feminist group, Redstockings, was known as Kathie Sarachild. Jewish women sometimes use the Hebrew form of "daughter of"—thus Deborah Bat Ruth: Deborah, daughter of Ruth. In this way, they are acknowledging matrilineal descent as the legitimate line. This attitude was made clear in a letter to the editor of the *San Francisco Chronicle*, October 28, 1976:

> There are many of us across the country who take seriously the connotation of "son" or "man" in our surnames and have chosen to modify or change them. My own case is an example. In 1974, I legally changed my name from P. E. Johnson to P. E. Lauradaughter. I view it as a declaration of independence—for myself—refusing to identify myself in the traditional patriarchal manner and terms. I am no one's "son" and I don't know who John is anyway. I do know Laura, my mother, and I credit her with much of my strength to celebrate my woman-ness in a society where woman-hating is part of the basic fabric.
>
> P. E. Lauradaughter

Other feminists take the name of the city in which they were born. Judy Chicago, for example, is a well-known feminist artist and author, one of the guiding spirits behind Womanhouse in Los Angeles. Other women take names from nature, such as Sage, Dawnspirit, Amber.[2] In doing so, they are reasserting their identification with the precivilization aspects of life. The changing of given names to those more in keeping with the newly emerging identity is not a widespread practice statistically; the fact that it is often done, and even done legally, testifies to the depth of the women's commitment to a new identity in an emerging cultural context.

2. The practice of taking names from nature as an indication of a new identity was widespread among hippies in the Haight-Ashbury district of San Francisco beginning in 1966. Feminists, in doing so, are emphasizing a bond that women have with forces of nature, and are thereby reaffirming aspects of cultural feminism.

As feminism and lesbian-feminism became widespread in the late 1960s many women began to make a political statement through their choice of clothing. A famous demonstration against the "rigid dictates of femininity" took place when outraged feminists threw false eyelashes, girdles, padded bras, and curlers into trash cans during the 1968 annual Miss America contest at Atlantic City. As the Women's Liberation branch of the movement began to identify with nationalist liberation movements, many of its members began to wear military dress in public. This was at a time in which mini-skirts and heavy makeup were fashionable. The contrast of these women who chose to dress asexually inspired other women to wean themselves away from the apparent security of traditional feminine dress (Kushner, 1974, p. 58).

Among lesbians, the extreme forms of male dress that "old gay" butches had adopted became modified as feminist thought influenced the lesbian community. As one lesbian pointed out in a 1971 interview about lesbian dress: "We're breaking down the old butch-femme roles which mimic heterosexual society. We're getting through all those layers and becoming real" (Haley, 1971).

Feminist and lesbian-feminist clothing is virtually indistinguishable except for subtle indications in dress or accoutrements. The dress for both groups begins with a body that is clean, healthy, unshaven, unbleached, and without makeup. Feminists may wear no underclothing at all, except possibly panties. Most women, unless they have uncomfortably large breasts, do not wear bras, which they say artificially distort and enhance the natural shape of the breast. The women who cultivate such a natural appearance are refusing to conform to the "degrading artifice" which the male-oriented culture dictates as appropriate, but which these women feel makes them into unwilling sex objects.

The outer garments that the women wear tend to become almost a uniform of utilitarian clothing. The women feel that in their choice of clothing they are striking a blow against the consumerism of a capitalist society as well as leveling class distinctions that might exist in the community. Their clothing mostly comes from "free boxes," in which people discard their still usable clothing to be recycled by anyone who wants it; from secondhand and army surplus stores; and from flea markets. Typical clothing consists of levis or other sturdy pants, T-shirts, workshirts, and as a top layer in cooler weather, heavy wool shirts or utilitarian jackets. Heavy hiking boots or tennis shoes are the usual footgear, and a rather endearing trait is the use of inexpensive boy's socks, often mismatched. Many women wear sunglasses or tinted prescription glasses, earrings, rings, and bracelets. Hair is worn long or short, but it is not artificially treated.

The women's self-presentation often contains subtle indications that they may be lesbians. At the time fieldwork was conducted, many lesbians wore short, layered "unisex" haircuts, lavender-tinted aviator glasses, and cowboy or combat boots. For the militant lesbian, there are other signs that she is a lesbian and proud of it. One such indication is handmade jewelry in the form of two symbols of the female intertwined, ♀♀, a widely recognized symbol of lesbianism. Often this symbol is on rings, belt buckles, or buttons. Special buttons are also worn for signification. A lavender star is one that is recognizable among gay liberation followers; the star is a recognized sign of liberation, and lavender signifies a gay identity. Other buttons contain graphic slogans such as "Dyke" or "Kiss me, I'm a Lesbian." Some women also wear men's vests, sometimes with men's ties and a "macho" hat, usually a man's hat from a secondhand store.

An article in the paper *Dykes and Gorgons* (1973), put out by the Gutter Dyke Collective in the East Bay, describes the significance of dress to the author.

> For me, dressing like a dyke has been wearing my inside feelings for the outside world to see.... Until the last few thousand years, all of the positive traits, now defined as male, were attached to women. The negative male attributes have since been labeled "feminine" until we've come to believe it ourselves. In order to reverse the process, we must try constantly to visualize ourselves in extremely positive and strong ways....
>
> Clothing traditionally made by men for women ... are designed to restrain women and keep them in a vulnerable position. They are physically harmful, shoddily made, and

6. *Two women watching a demonstration for Gay Rights. Note the "dyke" button. (The Bay Guardian: Rose Skytta)*

leave women wide open for rape and assault.... This leaves us with the choice of making all of our own clothing or by wearing the cheapest, sturdiest, and most protective clothing we can find that is already made....

The clothing we dykes wear today reflects our desire to identify as lesbians, to abandon male-defined "feminine dress," and to suit our own comfortability. We wear what makes us feel strong on the streets, gives us freedom of movement, and frees us as much as possible from sexist attacks by men.

Relationships

The pair relationship is the building block of the community, the ideal to which community members aspire. The nature of lesbian sexuality and love relationships are especially conducive to the egalitarian principles valued by community members. In order then to understand the particular characteristics of the lesbian-feminist couple, it is well to examine in detail the nature of lesbian sexuality, how it is translated into an emotional relationship, and how both of these aspects of lesbianism are affected by a feminist world view. Let us consider the close friendship between lesbian women, and how this affects the functioning of the community.

Sexuality

Since outsiders define the lesbian by her sexual preference, as opposed to the lesbian-feminist concept of the woman-identified-woman (p. 64), she is sometimes thought by them to be more sexual than most women. Some men have said that they fear the lesbian because they feel that, if given a chance, she will take their women away from them. Yet to them she is also a figure of male fantasy, since because of her alleged greater sexuality, she is thought to be a more tantalizing figure than the average woman; and because of her commitment to women she is more of a challenge to men. Many men secretly echo the sentiment about lesbians expressed in the phrase "All she needs is a good fuck." What this sentiment seems to imply is that with the right man (penis), the lesbian, more sexual, hence more challenging than other women, will abandon her lesbian preference and turn to men. Yet, there is the fear among some men that, because of her skill in lovemaking, if she ever has the opportunity to make love with their women, the women will find men to be inadequate lovers by comparison. The working-class father of one informant who later became a lesbian gave her the following advice when she went off to college: "Stay away from lesbians. They have a phenomenal sexuality. If you once experience it, you'll never want men."

Women in the community, however, stress that lesbians are not necessarily more sexual than other women. Yet there are reasons why many women prefer lesbian lovers to men. One is that lesbians, because they are women, are more likely to have the psychological and romantic needs common to women in love relationships, therefore they are more aware of the romantic, affectionate, tender aspects of a relationship—perhaps part of the nuturing role—than many men can allow themselves or know how to be. Lesbians, it has been said by informants, take time to reassure their lovers, to listen to them patiently, to be romantic without being embarrassed. As one woman exclaimed: "Lesbians are the most romantic people on earth!" This feeling is echoed in an article written by an anonymous lesbian about the lesbian experience:

> No one is more romantic than a lesbian in love. The reasons are simple. (1) First, she must continuously prove that she is *not* the vile creature society believes her to be. Consequently, she will outdo herself in display of "character" ... lavishly dispensing all the flowery appurtenances of love, rather than crudely emphasizing sex.... (2) The lesbian also has to prove that anything a man can do, she can do just as well—or better. So you can be sure she'll give the affair all possible energy, time, emotion, imagination, money, romance, and techniques. (3) Since *all* women are acknowledged to be romantic creatures— craving attention, affection, warmth, tenderness, understanding—then two women together are apt to be *very* romantic indeed....
>
> Lesbians have their anniversaries, their "our songs," pet names, silly games, special places where they met, and all the rest. They revisit "the scene of the crime," remember Valentine's Day, make much of birthdays, holidays, and other occasions which help cement their loosely-tied relationships, and give them a needed sense of "family," "tradition," "belonging." (Anonymous, 1971, p. 178)

Not only do women seem to take more time, have more patience and awareness of the need for tenderness, attention, and romance in a relationship with another woman than men in general are thought to have, they also are often more aware of the specific needs of female lovemaking techniques than men. As Kinsey points out, men biologically are more genitally oriented during sexual arousal than women, whose needs are more diffuse. Given this difference, Kinsey states that males use their own kind of psycho-sexual patterns to court women. "Most males are likely to approach females as they, the males, would like to be approached by a sexual partner. . . . They are inclined to utilize a variety of psychological stimuli which may mean little to most females" (1953, p. 466).

In general, a woman can know from her own sexual responses what is exciting to another woman during lovemaking. Women who have had sexual experiences with men as well as with women often comment that the nongenitally-focused sex that they have experienced with lesbians can be more exciting to them, since it gives them the time to build up completely to an orgasmic and often multi-orgasmic stage. Lesbian lovemaking has also been claimed by some lesbian-feminists to be inherently egalitarian, since each partner can take turns pleasing the other and no one partner needs to dominate.

Heterosexual lovemaking, by contrast, is thought to reinforce male dominance. Men are also thought by many lesbians to be inherently clumsy lovers. As one lesbian said: "If *lesbians* would teach men how to make love to women, there would never again be an unsatisfied sister."

Some men wonder what lesbians do with each other during lovemaking, since they may find it hard to imagine the lovemaking process without the involvement of a penis. A description offered by the anonymous author quoted above conveys a sense of lesbian lovemaking:

> What two women do together is very similar to heterosexual lovemaking. They take their clothes off, or they fumble around. They tease each other in cars or at the movies or under the table. They get in bed and caress, fondle, explore, kiss, suckle, and eventually, hopefully, experience orgasm. They may climax together or sepa-

rately. If lesbians are free-wheeling and imaginative, they may even think of extra sexual delights that men and women can't experience together. (Since lesbians are not limited by the problems of male potency, they can experience more orgasms in one session of lovemaking than would ever be possible during heterosexual intercourse.)

Granted, men are magnificently equipped to give women pleasure, but lesbians have their own ways of making up for the lack of a penis. They are adept at romantic talk, at taking time and displaying tenderness, and they have learned to use hands, mouths, and imaginations fully. In emotional and highly charged situations, these skills are more than enough to supply pleasure.... I think I can say most lesbians are good lovers because, as women, they know what other females want. And they are often more candid in telling each other what will please than men and women are with each other. Happy lesbians tend to be less intimidated and more intimate than heterosexual lovers, and this contributes to a good sex relationship. (p. 205)

It also contributes to a good love relationship. The fact that lesbians can be tender with each other in bed and that the nature of lesbian lovemaking can be inherently egalitarian means that, for many women, the trust and good feelings established during lovemaking carry over and help reinforce the emotional relationship. This works both ways: the trust in women that feminists have learned can help a lesbian couple who have a good emotional relationship have patience in working out a viable sexual relationship. It is worth noting that many lesbians keep close ties with former lovers, who become good friends. This seems to be less usual with heterosexual couples who break up.

Courting Patterns

Though an ideal for many lesbians is to be in a good pair relationship with another woman, there are difficulties in reaching this goal. These include the socialization patterns of the women involved, which may lead to anxiety and jealousy, a fear of being hurt, and a natural attrition in intimate relationships when the reality of daily life does not meet expectations.

91

According to informants, the texture of lesbian courtship differs in tempo from heterosexual patterns. Though women may make love with each other fairly soon in the relationship, the initial advances may take longer. And, since lesbians early learned the role expected of women in our culture, they tend to be more passive and more inhibited by possible rejection in making advances to another woman than men might be.[3]

One of the fears that a lesbian has when attracted to another woman is that the woman in whom she is interested is either heterosexual, bisexual, or, though affectually identifying herself as a lesbian, has never made love with a woman before. In each case, the fear of the lesbian approaching the woman is that she, herself, will be used. Among lesbians, there is verbal lore that heterosexual and bisexual women can't be trusted, that given the chance, they will leave the lesbian for a man. With the woman who is a self-identified lesbian but who has not yet had a physical experience with a woman, there is the fear that she will become more emotionally involved with the woman who brought her out" than is appropriate, or that she will have to be "mothered." On the other hand, there are thought to be advantages in bringing a woman out. It is said that a woman will be more faithful to the woman who brought her out than one fears a more experienced partner might be.

A woman who is interested in a possible love partner looks carefully for signs of responding interest before she approaches her. Some of the most widespread signs of interest are prolonged eye contact, smiling directly at someone, asking for a match, or indicating in some other way a heightened awareness of the other person. A common approach is asking a woman out for dinner, a movie, or to a women's dance.

Since many lesbians have little extra money for entertaining, the level of consumption during the evening is much different from what one might expect when out with a man who has access to more money. For one thing, many women are without cars and must depend on public transportation. An evening out

---

3. Contrary to the stereotype of the aggressive lesbian approaching a heterosexual woman, lesbians are very careful not to do that because they risk not only rejection but disclosure as well.

7. *A lesbian couple enjoying a day in the park together. (Virginia Morgan)*

with another woman is likely to focus more on conversation and walking and less on paid entertainment.

Though most women in the community say that they are look-ing for a long-term love relationship with a woman who is emo-tionally, intellectually, and sexually a partner in the fullest sense, in fact what is most typical of the lesbian community is "serial monogamy." A general pattern is being attracted to and getting to know a woman and, since there is no fear of pregnancy, making love early in the development of the relationship—this is known as "making the move"—and gradually getting into a "primary relationship." Sometimes there is a tension for a woman when she wants to be in a close relationship with the woman to whom she is most attracted, and also wants the free-dom to be open to other women. However, as the emotional momentum increases, the two women can become a couple and are recognized as such by the community. They may move in together or they may simply appear socially together and let their friends know that they are "with each other." Partly be-cause of their own needs for the relationship to succeed and partly because of the community's definition of them as a couple, they see themselves in a viable relationship and work to keep it going. As has been pointed out, the ideal relationship is defined as an egalitarian one in which each partner has emotional support from the other and yet each partner has the opportunity to develop her own fullest potential. In reality, most pair relationships do not reach this ideal, and usually, in time, the two women become emotionally involved with someone else, or they drift apart or formally break up.

The expectation, however, is to stay in a pair relationship and try to maintain it through the process of talking about the feelings of the partners and trying to reinforce a sense of commitment to the relationship. When there is finally a breakup, ideally the break is made in such a way that the former partners may remain friends.

It seems likely that, as many homosexuals of both sexes point out, in spite of the lack of legal and societal reinforcement of homosexual liaisons, there are probably relatively as many successful homosexual partnerships as there are heterosexual ones. The difference is that it is easier to dissolve homosexual liaisons that are not working out, so that their rate of attrition is higher. Many lesbian couples in the community have been together for up to two years, while some have been married in the common-law sense as long as twenty.

A major cause of breakups is jealousy. The feminist value of equality in establishing intimate relationships implies that there is no possessiveness. Sexual and emotional possessivenesses are thought to be politically incorrect, in that they are said by political members of the community to derive from two evils: capitalism, in which the lover is regarded as a possession who, if she is attracted to someone else, devalues the first relationship; and the nuclear family situation, in which children learn patterns of loving and have to compete for love within a very restricted group. Much of the struggle in lesbian relationships concerns working through feelings of anxiety, possessiveness, and jealousy with the partner. A member of the community talks about this process:

> What happened with [my] relationships was that from 1968 on, I was beginning to see that the ways in which I was

being with other women were neurotic and dependent and modeled a lot on heterosexual relationships. What being with women now means to me, after getting in touch with this well of sisterhood . . . is that I don't know that I cannot be jealous, but I don't want to feel that any one person is so necessary to me that I possess her and I do not want to feel possessed by any one person. . . . It's not so much that I'm rid of jealousy. . . . It's a way for me of handling it, accepting it, and realizing that it's a residue from another kind of living and trying to act on that knowledge, which does mean struggle sessions. . . .

Q: What happens if the woman with whom you're in a primary situation (a paired love relationship) gets turned on and acts on it?

A: That depends on how that alters her relationship to me. And if it alters her relationship to me in any significant way, then that's something we've got to struggle with. . . . As long as it does not, that other relationship tends to become a primary relationship in and of itself, I simply feel that's the kind of freedom that every human being ought to have. She grows because of it, I grow because of it, the other people grow because of it. Where it gets really hairy is where the romantic thing enters—when the outside relationship becomes more serious, or infatuation, and somehow it's hard to separate when this primary relationship has to take that into account.

Q: How do you do that?

A: Either I have to establish some kind of relationship with that third party—and that's not always possible, because I don't necessarily like the same kinds of people—or we have to work out some kind of "arrangement" just at a practical level—which really doesn't work much either. Or we have to say: "Okay, maybe it's time for this primary relationship to suspend itself and see where it is that you want to live through there, and maybe it's something permanent and I'll respect that fact that that may be it."

Q: If that happens, how do you deal with your own feelings?

A: Cry a lot . . . . I think I'd be really, really hurt and at a part of myself that's really legitimate, not just the part that's projecting and possessing, which I guess all of us still do to some extent. And a real sense of the loss of the kind of comfort that a primary relationship has. I would feel a little at loose ends, until one of my other relationships became primary, or I decided that I wanted to be alone, literally, for awhile, or to relate to a lot of people, none of them primary—this includes making love or having that option . . . . If the primary relationship I'm in now ceased to be a primary relationship, I would still want to relate on some levels, or at least have good feelings about that person. The whole serial monogamy thing was going thus far with a relationship and then cutting it off because you found someone else. I don't want to lose people who have been close to me anymore.

Finally, the tension between the proper political attitude of not wanting to possess another person, and the feelings of emotional bonding which seem to elicit a tendency toward such desires, are illustrated in a poem by Pat Parker, a well-known local poet.

A Small Contradiction
It is politically incorrect
   to demand monogamous
      relationships —
It's emotionally insecure
   to seek
      ownership of
   another's soul —
      or body &
damaging to one's psyche
to restrict the giving and
      taking of love.
   Me, i am
totally opposed to
monogamous relationships
      unless
         i'm
      in love.

Child of Myself

Members of the community, then, see themselves as a transitional generation, as pioneers, carrying with them the baggage of capitalism and patriarchal culture, but possessing the insights and determination to overcome the crippling emotional effects of that background. Their responsibility, they feel, is to struggle with their destructive emotions and try to establish new and better patterns for emotional relationships.

Friendships

Though the pair relationship is an ideal to which members of the community aspire, the more permanent and stable relationships are between close friends who are not lovers though they may have been lovers at one time. Close friends celebrate special occasions and holidays with each other and their lovers. Over the years, the lovers may change, but the close friendships usually remain fairly constant. The function of the close friend is that of kin: the close friend is the sister who will stick with one through the vicissitudes of life and to whom one can go at any time for support, advice, money, or companionship.

A woman may have one close friend who is her confidante, or she may be part of a small group of friends in a collective. Such friends keep in touch with each other daily by telephone, by visits, or by inquiring about the feelings, activities, and whereabouts of absent friends, to whom the message is relayed. Long telephone calls are often a part of the daily life of community members; their purpose is to share news of community activities or friends and to reinforce the social relationship.

There is a tacit understanding about the amount of time and attention friends spend with each other, either talking on the telephone or visiting. One woman, who went back to school full time, found that she was unable to maintain her usual degree of social participation. She was asked by her closest friends if something was wrong with the friendship, since the amount of time and attention she paid to the maintenance of the friendship had decreased. When I asked about this, one of her friends explained to me that lesbians take friendships very seriously, spend a lot of time cultivating and maintaining them, and are alert to signs of change in the quality of relationships. This is not surprising, since for most lesbians close friends are a substitute kin, their strongest support group. Lovers may come and go; consanguineal relatives are usually no longer a significant part of their emotional life; but friendships are the core of their personal support group, and as such serve a crucial psychological and emotional function.

Living Patterns

Though there is no formal geographic boundary for the San Francisco lesbian community, the women do tend to live in certain ethnically mixed, older, working-class areas of the city: Bernal Heights, the Mission district, the Castro area, and the Haight-Ashbury. These areas bound each other and have in common a quality of neighborhood life, low-rent housing, and the possibility of maintaining a kind of anonymity. These areas are accessible by public transportation to other parts of the city. Several of the seven lesbian bars in San Francisco are located in these neighborhoods, while most of the community projects are nearby.

Since the lesbian community is relatively poor and has a built-in degree of transience—much like a community of college students—one finds that most of the women live in old apartment buildings or small, low-rent houses. Very few women in the community own their own homes, though this is an often-stated goal for many of them.

The interiors of the apartments tend to be furnished with secondhand furniture, books, and records. Rooms are decorated with houseplants and with posters depicting feminist, lesbian, or aesthetic subjects. Most women have few possessions, and if they move they may leave some of these behind for roommates who choose to stay, since too great an attachment to material possessions is thought to be a remnant of capitalist thinking.

There is a large turnover in living arrangements in the community. Most of the women in the community are on marginal incomes. When a building is sold, or if there is no lease, the owner may raise the rent to the extent that the women can no longer afford it and are forced to find new lodgings at a lower rate. Many women also feel that if the landlord finds out that they are lesbians they will be asked to move. Therefore, one goal in the community is to have several apartment buildings owned by community members who will then rent safe housing at reasonable rates to other lesbians.

Aside from financial considerations, one reason for a fairly large turnover in living arrangements is that women who are lovers often live together. When they break up, one or both of them may want to move away from a place that has unhappy associations. But there is always pressure to turn vacated apartments over to other lesbians. Where several women are sharing a house or an apartment, there may be a shift in occupancy as one woman moves in with her lover; or it may develop that those sharing the house are not as compatible as it first appeared, and the whole household may break up, the members soon being absorbed into new living arrangements.

There are various ways in which a woman may hear about a vacancy in a lesbian household. The most obvious is through friends. Word-of-mouth transmission can occur in group situations, in which it is assumed that if a woman is participating, even if she is not known personally, she shares common values. In a group such as a feminist health-care session, one woman may announce that a vacancy is coming up. A third method is through public notices addressed to specific groups. Often these vacancy notices will specify "gay woman" or "lesbian roommate" wanted. These notices appear in the women's coffeehouses, bookstores, ice cream shops, and other places in which it is assumed the nature of the clientele will justify them.

The central clearinghouse for rentals in the community, however, is the San Francisco Women's Centers and Switchboard bulletin board. Several women have reported coming to San Francisco with no personal contacts, calling up the switchboard or checking their bulletin board, and following up on a request for a lesbian roommate. Through this one contact they have been able to become part of a social network and integrated into the community in a short time.

Since much of the socializing in the community consists of visiting friends, women without cars try to live near each other, so that gradually, within a small radius, many lesbian households may exist. One woman told me proudly that within the two-year period that she and her lover had lived at their present address, twelve lesbian households were established in a one block area nearby through word-of-mouth alone.

When a woman answers a notice or follows up on the news

that there is a vacancy in a lesbian household, she usually is invited over informally to see if she will fit into the household. For houses more politically oriented, this is of primary importance, for the members of the household are committed to welding the occupants of the house together as a collectivity. If she seems compatible, she is invited to move in.

The smallest living unit in the community is the single lesbian who lives alone but participates in community activities and is attached to a social network, some of whose members may be couples. She may live alone by choice, feeling that her personal needs are best met this way, or she may simply still be in the process of trying to find a lover or a roommate. The next smallest unit is a couple who live together with no one else in the house. A variation of the couple pattern is the lesbian mother who lives with her lover and her children, or two lesbian mothers who are lovers and who share a place with both their families. However, since many lesbian mothers are wary of the effects of nuclear family life on their children, they may prefer to live with a lover, their children, and at least one other adult to whom their children can relate as a kind of extended kin (see chapter five).

For politically oriented women, to whom forging a collectivity is an important part of their ideology, the "house"—a living arrangement of several women who are committed to and active in the same politics and who carry their politics over into how the house is run—is the ideal. The women may be not only a living collective in that they share equally the expenses and chores involved in running the house and work toward forging a sense of collectivity among house members, they may be a working collective as well.

The house as a political unit serves several functions. It is a living space and can be a sanctuary for its members from the outside world. It is also a model for a small community in which the process of collective living is practiced. It is a political unit, and as such, it is the arena in which the members are exposed to a constant reinforcement of egalitarian collective principles.

Most houses have four to eight members, who share a commitment to develop the house as a collectivity. People who live in such houses come to be known by their membership in them, so the way in which a particular house is regarded in the community can color the view of its individual members. When a crisis arises, for example, whoever is organizing action to deal with it contacts those houses which she knows will want to be involved, and the house as a unit turns over its energies for that purpose. Similarly, houses will hold social events with other houses as collectivities, such as "their house is coming over for dinner." Though individual members have other social identities and ties, the emphasis in the community is for the political house to function as a unit.

Still other women may live together in an apartment but without a political framework. Some live in mixed groups; for example, a lesbian may live with two gay men and a heterosexual mother of two children. Her social involvement is directed toward the lesbian community; her housing arrangement is merely expedient.

The housing arrangements made by women in the community depend on how politically involved they are, whether they are in a pair relationship and how they define it, the income they have, and the kind of housing that is available. But housing serves more than a merely utilitarian function; how and with whom the women live defines to some extent their social identity within the collectivity.

Working Patterns

Working patterns, like housing patterns, can be pragmatic, but they also function to underline the social identity of the women involved. Since their values stress antimaterialism, most women in the community choose not to compete for high-salaried, professional jobs, which they equate with middle-class, capitalistic values. It is a subsistence community, for many by choice. Members prefer to use their time and energy for political projects and activities, rather than to pursue typical careers. From the data, working patterns fall into several categories. There are those women to whom participation in the community has a higher priority than earning an income. These women are eligible for and are on government assistance programs, or take part-time "shitwork" jobs in order to devote time and what extra money they have to community projects. Then there are women who are learning skills or developing expertise in more traditional jobs, but who define what they are doing as "ripping off the system." They plan to use their training for the benefit of the community. These women may be attending college or graduate schools or are apprenticed, learning blue-collar skills. Finally, there are women who work full time, perhaps in a closeted condition, sometimes supporting lovers in the first two categories, and who donate part of their larger income for community projects. For them, their participation in the community takes place during their hours off the job.

Because of the nature of the community work patterns, there are inherent strengths and weaknesses. One of the advantages is that, since success at a professional level is not important to most members, there is personnel available to carry out community projects and to participate in activities on a continuing basis. However, because this is not a community of professionally trained and employed people, projects often risk floundering because money is not available or the skills necessary to maintain them have not been developed.

As we have seen, the goal for community members is to have enough women skilled and sharing their skills so that the community can be entirely self-sufficient and separated from the larger community. It is envisioned that women will have their own healers, their own artists, their own crafts people, their own builders and maintenance people. In short, in common with many poor and oppressed communities, it is hoped that the training and knowledge of any member will ultimately be channeled toward the good of the community.

Leisure Time

Since the community consists largely of women who are not living with a family, the use of their leisure time is characteristic of young adults without family responsibilities. Most of the women prefer to spend their leisure time with friends, with lovers, with other members of the community, and if they do go out into the larger social world of San Francisco—for example, to see a movie downtown—it is with another member or in a group.

As was mentioned before, many community members are on marginal incomes, therefore entertainment expenses cannot be large. There are periodic social events that cater to lesbian-feminists, such as benefit performances by lesbian singers, all-women's dances at which women's bands play, and occasional speeches by nationally known lesbian-feminists, with parties afterward. Political demonstrations also function as social events in that women often meet there and socialize afterwards. Demonstrations are held whenever there are events of concern to the community, such as support for lesbian mothers' cases.

Places in the community in which to spend leisure time include the two women's coffeehouses, where community members feel free to drop in and spend an afternoon or an evening; the seven women's bars, which have the feel of neighborhood bars and in which the regular clientele is known; and bookshops, either specifically women's bookstores or small, alternative bookstores where one can hang out for a couple of hours without feeling pressured to buy something.

There is also a very active sports calendar for women who want either to participate or to watch. Every year several of the women's bars sponsor baseball teams made up of regular habitués. Women who go to the bars regularly go to the public playgrounds to watch the games and root hard for their team. There is a lot of interest in and support for these games and some bars even have elaborate uniforms and cheerleaders. The league is not restricted to the city of San Francisco alone; teams from the East Bay also participate. These games last most of the afternoon, and women who come to watch meet old friends, relax, drink beer, and root for their team. There are often children of the players or the fans present and the feeling is of a pleasant relaxed way to spend a sunny afternoon, with a lot of social interaction, friendly conversation, conducting of business, and flirtation going on in the stands. After the games, many women go to the winning team's bar to continue the celebration. Sometimes the bars have free drinks or even free meals to celebrate winning. The bars also sponsor pool tournaments, which have a large following. Among the regulars, women are known by how well they play, and many women practice for hours to sharpen their skill.

A large number of women play baseball and, to a lesser extent, other team sports on a less organized basis than the bar league. It is often a question of a telephone call or two to a house in which the members are likely to play, to get a game together. Sometimes, in the summertime, there may be games several times a week.

The bars also sponsor social events. There are periodic parties, such as a birthday party each month for all the women whose astrological sign is represented by that month. There are annual picnics, which are held out of town and which several dozen women attend for game competition, to eat picnic food, and to relax and play. Through these activities, habitués of bars get to know each other in a slightly different context, while the concept of the bar becomes more personalized and less strictly materialistic. Although the bars and their related activities are used by many lesbian-feminists for socializing, they still represent social patterns more in keeping with old gay life—cruising, role-playing, and more superficial relationships. They are not feminist environments, though feminists go there from time to time.

Most entertaining in the community is done in women's homes. Women who live in houses arrange to have a night when they can invite friends over for dinner, or the entire house may invite another house over, all members contributing to the dinner. Women living alone might ask another woman over, either as an act of friendship or perhaps as the start of a more serious involvement. There are advantages to entertaining at home: it is less expensive and the women are less likely to be annoyed by outsiders or intruded on by friends or acquaintances. If women do eat out, they tend to go to small restaurants in the neighborhoods in which they live.

There are other characteristic uses of leisure time. In general, community members advocate personal growth as well as physical fitness—partly for the sake of survival. Therefore, activities and crafts such as macrame, photography, writing, painting, playing musical instruments, tai-chi, yoga, meditation, furniture building, auto and motorcycle mechanics, are all widespread in the community. Many members do not attend traditional schools, but they work hard to develop skills and interests on their own, often trading off lessons in one skill for information about another.

Some leisure time is spent with pets. It seems to be a pattern for lesbians without children to have an unusually high number of pets—cats, dogs, mice, birds—soft creatures who respond when a woman comes home, something to cuddle and talk to, particularly when other people are unavailable. This may be a widespread pattern with single urban-dwellers in general, but it is very prevalent in the lesbian community.

Leisure time is also used to nurture relationships. Since it is a community in which emotions are taken seriously, and since the members function as kin to each other, a lot of time is spent on long phone calls to find out what is happening with other community members, to keep in touch with close friends and acquaintances daily, to try to make a friendship closer, to work out misunderstandings, to break up, to explain to other friends why a couple broke up—in short, to keep up with and add to the current emotional pattern of community life.

It is characteristic that almost all use of leisure time takes place within community boundaries. If these boundaries are transcended, the women seem to be less relaxed, and usually arrange to go to outside events with at least one other member, thus carrying the safety of the community into the outside world.

4. COMMUNITY PROJECTS

The lesbian-feminist community has access to projects and facilities that exist on the boundaries of the self-contained collectivity. Many of these are not specifically addressed to lesbians, but rather are geared to the larger community of feminist women. However, for all but the most extreme lesbian separatists, these are "legitimate" places to go, since they were initiated and are run by women, some of them lesbians. Therefore, lesbians do use these facilities and define them as part of their social universe. These facilities offer crisis counseling, legal services, health care, financial aid, employment facilitation, feminist educational programs, art projects, child-care, recreation, and they include the Women's Centers, a women's switchboard, seven bars, two coffeehouses, bookstores, and publishing services.

Many of these projects in the larger community of women, though not run entirely by lesbians, are strongly influenced by the lesbian-feminists who staff them. The inception and the recruitment of staff for most, if not all, of these projects take into consideration an ideology (a commitment to feminism or lesbian-feminism), individual interests (the personality, skills, and particular interests of the women involved), and action (participation in the project, including the way the project is structured). Thus, the more political women in the community, those who see the struggle as within a class context involving working-class and third-world women as well as lesbians, focus on this group. Women whose skills are in health-care fields might band together to combat what they define as male-dominated, hierarchichal medical care by running a women's health clinic with a focus on preventive medicine. Women who have no special training and whose political commitment is more loosely defined in that they "just want to help other women" can volunteer to work on the Women's Switchboard. Women who see the focus of lesbian-feminism as cultural might teach courses in women's history, research some aspects of women's culture, or develop environments in which cultural modes are reinforced.

In this chapter two projects that represent the first steps toward a self-sufficient lesbian-feminist community are compared in detail. These two projects are significant as a demonstration of the range of possibilities inherent in the lesbian-feminist community. They were both initiated by collectives made up of lesbian-feminists (one of them originally included a heterosexual feminist, but she dropped out). Both projects went through a process of redefinition and reformation as the politics implicit in them were rigorously tested. They represent vividly different ideological points of view within the larger spectrum of lesbian-feminism. Because of their differences, a comparison of the projects is helpful in documenting the strengths and weaknesses of the community. Since anonymity is necessary, the two projects have been given fictitious names. For the purpose of this book they will be referred to as Demeter's Daughters, the women's coffeehouse and bookstore, and the Women's Training Center. Even the original concepts of these projects demonstrate deep differences in outlook between their two founding collectives.

Demeter's Daughters was conceived by middle-class lesbian-feminists who were introduced to feminist ideology in women's studies at a local university. It was an extension of this literary and cultural context that the collective was formed and the coffeehouse and bookstore ultimately established. The only political decision the members of the collective had made was to open the establishment to all women. Since the women involved had not had any experience with the divisiveness that could be inherent in an activity in which shades of political differences, expectations, and responsibilities had not been worked out explicitly in advance, they were unprepared when a split developed within the organization. In the end, the founding collective retained control over the project, while its basic nature, an environment for the reinforcement of cultural feminism, was not affected. What did change was the method of running the coffeehouse, and this was altered so as to be more in keeping with the suggestions of some of the more political members of the community.

The Women's Training Center, on the other hand, had an entirely different kind of base and environment. Its founding collective was an all-lesbian group of very political, mostly working-class women, who felt that the greatest need in the community was skills for jobs. They felt that their enterprise addressed a more basic level of survival then Demeter's Daughters. They had designated responsibilities from the beginning and had incorporated discussion groups and small-group meetings to deal with dissatisfaction and change. Since their priorities were more strongly lesbian, working class, and third world, they had a different kind of clientele than Demeter's Daughters, though many women who used the center also went to the coffeehouse. When there was finally some dissension from a group of third-world women, the collective ultimately turned the entire project over to these women, thereby losing control over it but adhering to their principles.

Demeter's Daughters, then, was conceived by middle-class cultural feminists, and the Women's Training Center emerged from a collective of political, working-class women with a strong class analysis. With these distinctions in mind, let us turn to a more detailed description of the process by which each project was conceived, developed, and put into action, remembering that, different as they are, they both illustrate aspects of lesbian-feminist ideology.

Demeter's Daughters Coffeehouse and Bookstore

Because the coffeehouse and bookstore emphasized and reinforced the cultural aspects of feminism, a close examination of its decor and milieu will indicate the ways in which the decision to focus on the cultural theme was carried out. Unlike the Women's Training Center, which addressed itself to attacking opppression of women at an economic level, the coffeehouse was a total feminist cultural haven—a kind of oasis in a male-dominated world. All aspects of the coffeehouse reinforced a women's environment—the choice of books, the performers and their material, the art selected to hang on the walls, and the way in which the establishment was run.

History

Long before the formation of the Daughters of Bilitis in 1955, a need was felt for an alternative to the bars where women, and especially lesbians, might congregate. The idea of a woman's environment, where women could relax in comfortable, pleasant surroundings, with women's artwork, women performers, and women's literature all available in one place, removed from the strong role-playing demands of a mixed, male-dominated environment, has been a goal toward which to strive. In some ways, individual women's homes and the Daughters of Bilitis's discussion sessions had served this purpose, but only to a limited extent, and these facilities were not easily accessible to the larger community of women.

It was not until the opening of Demeter's Daughters on International Women's Day, March 7, 1974, that this goal was realized in San Francisco. The name, Demeter's Daughters, was chosen because the five women who made up the original collective had wanted a name that was mythical and that had connotations of a matriarchal place. The moon has always been identified as a symbol of women; to the Greeks and Romans the moon was governed by a goddess—Diana, Artemis, Cybele— and these connotations have remained in Western symbolism. The moon goddess has been identified, as well, with women's monthly cycles, and has a regenerative quality. As one of the founders described the process of naming the coffeehouse: "We were kicking around names and we wanted one that was mythic and represented women. Phyllis Chesler's book (*Women and Madness*) was lying on the table and we flipped through it and came to a passage about the moon:

> Artemis, the youngest of Demeter's daughters, returned to her mother's house. First, she had Demeter consecrate her to the moon, so that no matter how far she'd have to wander, she would never forget, never betray her origins. That done, Artemis quickly perfected the arts of hunting

and riding and warfare, of plant healing and midwifery. Then, with the moon for a guide, she left to found a city—no, it was a tribe—no, it was a culture, the likes of which the world had never known. Every woman in it was a soldier and a mother, tears were as common as physical bravery, marriage was scorned, rape unthinkable, and the love of young girls was praised in poems written by even the most hardened veterans. Artemis herself had many female lovers, and many daughters, each of whom founded other Amazon cities in Africa, in South America and elsewhere in Asia. (Chesler, 1972, p. xviii)

So we kept thinking of moon names, and of sisterhood, and finally I said: 'What about Demeter's Daughters?' Everybody liked it and we also asked other women in the community and they all liked it, so that's what the name was."

One of the members of the collective described (in a taped interview) how the undertaking developed:

We chose each other to begin with because we liked and respected each other and trusted each other implicitly. That's important. We made a personal commitment to each other to support each other if needed. That included pooling money, which is where many commitments stop. It was crucial to have that commitment to it and to each other. If one of us needs to get an outside job, someone else will take over her shifts. If we disagreed, we worked through it, rather than overlook it and have it come up later. We didn't have a strict business or a strict ideology in mind. We focused on getting the coffeehouse going, not on political ideology.

As was mentioned, the five women met each other while taking courses in women's studies. These courses, which began in 1970, were the first contact with the women's movement for most of the women in the Demeter's Daughters collective.

The five women who made up the collective decided to open a coffeehouse, but first they had to learn how to do it. They went to other coffeehouses and specialized bookstores and asked technical questions. Financing devolved on the members of the collective and some came from personal loans from friends.

Help and advice came from members of the community who had specialized knowledge. By the time the coffeehouse opened, many women who had never worked in the community, as well as activists who had a great deal of relevant experience, had worked on the project, thus creating a sense of participation and solidarity from community members from the start.

Structure

The coffeehouse is open six days a week, from four to midnight on weekdays, from noon to midnight on weekends. It is closed on Monday. This schedule has had repercussions in the rest of the community. For example, one of the women's bars nearby started serving coffee on Monday night so that this kind of facility would be available to the women's community even when Demeter's Daughters was closed. The Daughters of Bilitis, as well, out of an impulse to dovetail existing facilities, has moved its traditional weekly meeting night from Wednesday, when activities are sometimes scheduled at the coffeehouse, to Monday, when it is closed. Demeter's Daughters, in turn, tries not to hold events on the same evenings as those sponsored by other community projects.

Twenty-four volunteers staff the facility in four hour shifts. Though the five-member founding collective has the responsibility for ordering supplies and paying bills, an attempt is made to include these volunteers when decisions are made on how Demeter's Daughters is to be run. Many of these women have been regular volunteers since the coffeehouse opened. They need other sources of income, such as part-time jobs, to be able to live while devoting time to the coffeehouse. Because current bills have to be paid, and some of the original funding was from personal loans that must be paid off, the volunteers are not (at this writing) on a salary. The five-woman collective hopes to be able to pay these women and is working on ways of doing so. Though volunteers sometimes trade off shifts or get substitutes when they are unable to come, the volunteer system works because of the dedication of the women involved. Volunteers who are not reliable, or who are unhappy with the way in which the project is run, drop out, and new volunteers are recruited from regular customers.

The organizing principle of the coffeehouse is to run it as a collective endeavor serving the larger community of women. Three kinds of meetings are held regularly: Informal meetings of the five-member collective deal with things directly in their purview, such as the priority for paying bills. Larger meetings are held with the core collective and the volunteers. It is here that grievances are brought up and suggestions are made, discussed, and worked out in this context. The third kind of meeting involves all women in the larger community who want to participate. These meetings are infrequent and they are announced in the monthly calendar so that women can plan to come and speak up, knowing that their suggestions will be considered and incorporated if feasible. In this way, the staff tries to be responsive to the needs of the larger community.

However, because the coffeehouse was established before there was a comprehensive political analysis of how it was to be run, when there finally was some dissension on the part of volunteers who wanted more voice in making decisions, there was no organized way to deal with the situation. It was resolved finally with the help of a professional feminist mediator, who used the techniques of collective decision-making with both sides, the dissenting volunteers and the core collective members, discussing the points of disagreement on both a personal level and a political level. After several mediating sessions, both sides decided to bring the problem to the larger community. They held an open meeting for the entire women's community in which each side presented a position paper and each spoke about its interpretation of the situation. Finally, there were questions and comments from the floor. There was strong feeling about the split among members of the larger community and questioning became rather pointed.

The outcome was that several of the most adamant volunteers left to form their own collective, which became a political study group, and other women took their places. The original small collective then tried to open its decision-making to all the volunteers who wanted to be part of it. Thus, when the dissension was brought out into the open and to the attention of the larger community, the way in which the coffeehouse was run was altered from a pattern that had developed arbitrarily as needs arose to a more truly democratic decision-making process.

However, there was still some criticism from former volunteers and some community members whose politics differed from that of the small collective.

Description

The coffeehouse and bookstore is located on the ground floor of the building in which it is housed. It is three blocks from the main street of a bustling neighborhood served by several bus and streetcar lines. It is in an area with a fairly low crime rate, which is an important consideration for a place with a female clientele. The location of the coffeehouse contributes to its success, for it is near the areas of the city in which most members of the community live, Noe Valley, Bernal Heights, the Mission district, and the Haight-Ashbury. Only a small stenciled sign on the front window indicates that the building houses a women's coffeehouse. Though it has large front windows, these are screened off for the sake of privacy. The women who go there want to be able to relax in an atmosphere away from men and do not want passing men staring in at them.

The interior reinforces the feminist environment and invites use for community needs. As one enters the coffeehouse, the first thing visible is a "free box," an innovation developed in the counterculture, in which still usable clothes are available to anyone who wants them. Bulletin boards on which any woman can put up announcements or advertisements are on the walls. Most of the signs are requests for roommates, appeals for other women to participate in a particular enterprise, and announcements of events of interest to the community. For example, an announcement of a benefit to raise money for the Women's Training Center was prominently featured. The bulletin board is one of the few contacts isolated women have with the community. A much more comprehensive listing is available through the Women's Switchboard and on bulletin boards at the Women's Centers, but many women come to the coffeehouse before they know about the other facilities. On the wall is also the monthly calendar of events of the coffeehouse itself. A table is available for petitions for specific causes addressed to the feminist community, so that the required number of signatures can be obtained quickly.

113

The coffeehouse itself is in a long, rather narrow room, running the length of the building. There are windows on the back wall, providing light and ventilation. The overall impression is one of comfort, a cozy place in which one can spend several hours pleasantly. There is usually an exhibit of paintings or drawings by local women artists. The works are for sale at reasonable prices so that women on small incomes can afford to buy them. Often Demeter's Daughters is the first place that women artists are able to show and sell their work. The art reinforces a feminist atmosphere; the subjects of the work are often loving and skillful portrayals of women being tender with each other, portraits of friends, and sometimes caricatures of forms of male oppression.

The interior of the coffeehouse was completely renovated by volunteers from the community who taught each other construction skills or learned them together. The furniture consists of round, varnished tables made of cable spools, with fresh flowers on them, and a motley assortment of chairs gathered from wherever they were available. The Daughters of Bilitis donated several metal folding chairs, which are useful for the larger audience that appears on nights when there is entertainment. There are also many green plants, which add to a hospitable and pleasant environment. A donated piano is available for anyone to play. The low platform which serves as a stage is in one corner; when not in use it is covered by large pillows to sit on. The only overt sign of lesbian influence is on a gate to the kitchen: a hand-carved heart with the signs for female entwined.

Food

The large kitchen has a counter from which food is served. Customers come up to the counter and order what they want; there is no table service. Most women carry their plates and cups back to the counter when they have finished, to make less work for the staff. The coffeehouse tries to feature food that is nourishing and inexpensive. A lot of thought went into the kind of food served in the coffeehouse, since there is concern in the women's community about eating properly on a minimum income. In light of this, there is a house policy that no woman shall ever be refused food or drink because she has no money to pay for it.

The Bookstore

Near the entrance to the building is a small room that serves as the bookstore, and bookshelves take up most of the space. Browsing is encouraged, and there is a chair to sit on while reading. A sign on the door reminds the customers: "Women writers need your support."

The stock of the bookstore, like the environment of the coffeehouse, makes a political statement by reinforcing a feminist atmosphere. The books are either by or about women. Paperback editions make up the bulk of the stock, since women in the community want to read and buy books and most of them cannot afford the more expensive editions. The types of books offered include fiction, poetry, health care, self-defense, autobiographies and biographies of feminists, and analyses of women's legal, educational, economic, and political situations. Many local poets are featured. Feminist and lesbian-feminist journals and newspapers from all over the country are regularly stocked. The bookstore has the largest collection of this material in San Francisco.

There are a few records by feminist or lesbian singers. Until recently women who felt romantic about other women had no songs with which to express their feelings. It was not until women themselves began to write, sing, and record their own music that a few feminist and more specifically lesbian songs became available to the public. Other records, while not romantic, reflect sentiments of the movement. Jewelry made by women artisans is also for sale; this jewelry can be used during ritual gift-exchange celebrations. By wearing it, a woman openly identifies herself as part of the community.

The bookstore also sells a few items of clothing specifically designed for its clientele. One example is a yellow tank-top with a purple star in the middle (signifying gay liberation) and the word "Superdyke." This shirt was designed and made by two local women. It has become very popular in the community, and the bookstore is one of the few places in which it is available.

The walls of the bookstore are covered with posters and a few prints for sale. Their content strongly reiterates a commitment to feminism. By buying and displaying these posters, one reinforces an identification with the ideology they express. The subject matter of the posters ranges, but all of it reflects feminist and

8a/8b. The interior of a feminist bookstore. A display of T-shirts with slogans supporting lesbianism, third world struggles, and ecology. Note the "Superdyke" shirt. (Virginia Morgan)

lesbian-feminist concerns. One very popular poster is about lesbianism. It is a photograph of two women asleep in a brass bed, with a sign on the wall above them saying "Lesbians Unite." The slogan on the poster, a double entendre, is "Sisterhood Feels Good."

There are also small drawings that carry out a lesbian theme. One shows three female nude figures, drawn without features; two of these are adult, the third is a child. The drawing is a representation of a lesbian family, which serves children of a lesbian mother as an alternative model to the nuclear family so often depicted in the media.

Other concerns of the women's movement are also represented by posters. One of these is the martyrdom of the estimated nine million women who were burned as witches because, it is said, they were atypical of the narrow definition of the role of women in the historical epoch in which they lived. Many contemporary women think that these women were lesbians (see p. 25). Feminists today have resurrected the memory of these women, who are seen not as malevolent witches but as followers of Wicca, a religion of the Mother Goddess. This particular poster depicts a thoughtful-looking woman, and the slogan reads: "I saw witches in my front burner/recriminate/and silent/glowing out of flames/at Salem." It should be pointed out that some feminists see the entire history of the patriarchy as a general persecution of women by men; and, since men controlled the recording of history, this theme was lost. Only in extreme cases, such as the burning of large numbers of women, are there some signs of this history. In making explicit the history of oppressed people, such victims' visibility is important.

Other posters in the bookstore are more oriented toward action. Two of them are announcements for International Women's Day in March, which honors the massive organization among women in America for suffrage and in struggles for unionization. On March 8, 1857, women textile workers first marched to protest their working conditions. In 1910 at the Second International Conference of Socialist Working Women, the celebration of International Working Women's Day on March 8 was established. Until World War I, International Working Women's Day was celebrated in America and Europe, but the war caused its discontinuation. In 1968, feminists in Berkeley, learning about the history of working women, reinstated its celebration in the Bay Area San Francisco Women's Union (pamphlet, March 1975).

Another poster follows a similar theme. The slogan reads: "Yes, it is bread we fight for, but we fight for roses, too," from the workers' song "Bread and Roses."[1] Another poster is about rape as an act of violence against the oppressed. Its format is the front page of a newspaper, *The Forward Times*, which carries the headline "Women Declare War on Rape." The headlines for the stories carry out this theme.[2]

The last poster carries out the theme of the sisterhood of all women, which transcends class and race differences. It is a quote from one of a series of poems, *A Common Woman*, by a Bay Area poet with a national following among feminists, Judy Grahn, who writes about the lesbian experience as one of her themes. The excerpt on the poster is from the poem "Vera: From My Childhood," and has passed into lesbian-feminist and feminist folklore. It is used as a motto both in speech and on samplers and posters: "The common woman is as common/As a common loaf of bread ... And will rise!" It refers to the invincibility of woman even after a long history of oppression. The entire poem:

> Solemnly swearing, to swear as an oath
> to you who have somehow gotten to be a pale
> old woman; swearing, as if an oath could be
> wrapped around your shoulders like a new coat;

1. According to Marge Kenright, the librarian for the International Longshoremen's Union, Local 10, this song was inspired by the Lawrence Strike of January 1912, and first appeared in the form of a poem written by James Oppenheim.

2. Women Against Rape, or WAR, is a loose coalition of feminist rape-prevention squads in various cities. It is the closest thing the movement has to a women's army. Its enemy is a symbol of male supremacy, the rapist, who feels he is entitled to use violence to force women to submit to becoming objects for his "phallic gratification." The women in WAR function in the tradition of their conception of classical Amazons. They not only protect other women, they also comfort and advise them after they have been raped. They have set up a "hotline" telephone service, so that when a victim is raped, another woman will accompany her to the police and to the hospital for moral support.

For your 28 dollars a week and the bastard boss
you never let yourself hate;
And the work, all the work you did at home
Where you never got paid;
For your mouth that got thinner and thinner
until it disappeared as if you had choked on it,
watching the hard liquor break your fine husband down
into a dead joke.
For the strange mole, like a third eye
right in the middle of your forehead;
for your religion which insisted that people
are beautiful golden birds and must be preserved;
for your persistent nerve
and plain white talk—
the common woman is as common
as good bread
as common as when you couldn't go on
but did.
For all the world we didn't know we held in common
all along
The common woman is as common as the best of bread
and will rise
and will become strong—I swear it to you
I swear it to you on my own head
I swear it to you on my common
woman's
head.

Although there is a potential for shoplifting from the bookstore—since there is not enough volunteer staff to look after the needs of the bookstore as well as the coffeehouse when it is crowded—this does not often happen. The staff assumes that women who use the facility are committed to community values and will not steal from a woman's business. Sometimes women ask to take books they want home, promising to pay later. According to one of the staff, they usually do pay.

A Typical Evening

Members of the community are expected to support activities that are important to its growth. Therefore, whenever some

120

undertaking needs funds for a specific purpose, it either holds a fund-raising benefit or solicits individual donations. A recent evening's entertainment at the coffeehouse served both to raise funds and to introduce to the local community the work of a woman new to the area. The evening was described on the calendar as a poetry benefit night. Whenever a benefit night is planned, it is noted on the calendar with the amount of the expected donation so that women will know that if they are present and expect to stay during the entertainment, a basket will be passed for the donation. If they are not willing to donate, they are expected to leave to make room for women who will. The donations are split evenly between the house and the performers during non-benefit performances; for benefits, the performers receive the entire sum donated.

Usually such performances are on the weekends, when more women are able to attend. It is necessary to come early on these nights, since most performers have a large following and these performances are among the least expensive kinds of entertainment offered in the city. There are usually about ten donation nights scheduled monthly, though there is free entertainment at other times. There is also a monthly open-stage night for women who do not feel like performing for an entire evening but who want the experience of performing before an audience of women. Often such women do come back later to perform on regular nights.

Donation-night entertainment in April 1975 included a screening of the most recent work of a women's film company, a benefit for local women who were arrested during a feminist demonstration, poetry, blues, and an evening of classical piano. Three of the women featured as entertainers are nationally known. They entertain at Demeter's Daughters as a gesture of camaraderie to the local community and to maintain their ties with it.

The calendar also announces benefits held by other sponsors, who want community support. The major benefit in April was held at the Women's Training Center, and it was to help pay for the defense of a black woman prisoner who killed the white prison warden who she said raped her. Community solidarity is demonstrated by the fact that projects which often are dependent on the same clientele advertise each other's functions.

On one particular evening at Demeter's Daughters, because of the large following of the poet Judy Grahn, the coffeehouse was crowded long before eight o'clock when the first of two readings was scheduled to begin. Members of the audience moved about and greeted old friends in a generally relaxed atmosphere. About fifteen minutes before the reading was to begin, one of the staff of the coffeehouse passed around a basket for the dollar donations, informing people that there was going to be a show soon, and if they did not want to stay for it, they would be expected to leave.

At eight o'clock, Judy Grahn, a slender, dignified woman, who is self-identified as a lesbian, got up to open the evening's entertainment. She explained that the purpose of the evening was to raise part of the three hundred dollars needed to pay for paper to publish a book of essays written by the other woman who was to be introduced that evening. The collection would be published by the Women's Press Collective (later merged with Diana Press), whose list includes some fourteen titles of feminist and lesbian-feminist writers' works. The purpose of the collective is to present the writing of these women, who have difficulty being published by traditional houses, to as wide an audience as possible, to introduce new writers to their potential audience, and to give writers as much control over their own work as they can.

Judy Grahn mentioned that most women writers and artists have to work on a regular eight-hour-a-day job and that only in the evenings, after their other responsibilities are taken care of, do they have time to write. She then read from some of her own work, which was still in progress. Some of this material was a prose description of young Native American girls figuring out how to escape peril; a description of the talents of various wise women of the tribe; and a poem that eulogized a strong lesbian woman who endured. She was listened to with rapt attention and was applauded enthusiastically. Because of Judy Grahn's following in the community, women who had never before come to the coffeehouse attended the reading.

Judy Grahn introduced the second reader, a young heterosexual woman from the Southern mountains whose writing describes the experience of women living in the last bastion of Southern manhood. She read short sketches about people she had known as she grew up. The general subject was both the strength and the lack of opportunity of women who live in a subculture in which they are expected to get married while in high school. Her subject matter included being in love with a man and being badly treated by him. She too was listened to with attention.

When the reading ended, Judy Grahn announced that there would be a second reading and that the material would be different, and for those who wanted to stay it would be another dollar. As part of the audience filed out, she was at the exit to thank the people who had come. There was a small basket for further donations for the paper. Most of those who left contributed to it.

Clientele

It is estimated by the bookkeeper that in its first year the coffeehouse was used by more than fourteen hundred women. There is a core of regulars, which shifts in content and grows in absolute numbers. The collective feels that one of the limitations of the coffeehouse is that it is still largely used by white, middle-class women; third-world and working-class women who are feminists or lesbians either don't know about the facility or don't relate its existence to their own lives.

One of the collective members told me: "The joy of this place is that it's integrated [she meant that both lesbian and heterosexual women use it]. The bars are pickup places and places to dance and play pool. The bars are more threatening to straight women. Some bar women come here—they're not regulars— sometimes for special entertainment, sometimes for books." Other women, speaking in an open meeting, felt that the "bar women," because they are thought to have less commitment to feminist political identification and therefore do not necessarily view themselves as part of a larger community of women, do not come to the coffeehouse and would not feel comfortable there, since coffeehouse culture differs from bar culture. However, the same women, who are political activists, added, "We all go to the bars though."

At one of the open meetings, a woman suggested that Demeter's Daughters should be more lesbian-identified. As was noted earlier, originally it was to be open to "all women," and the founding collective adheres to this policy. What this woman referred to was the fact that when lesbians are expressing affection to each other, heterosexual women who are unused to this sometimes show surprise or discomfort. There are few other public places in which lesbian couples and friends can openly express affection, and they resent feeling inhibited in a place they have defined as one in which they should feel comfortable. Therefore, if heterosexual women were more alerted to the fact that they might find lesbians in the coffeehouse, there would be less awkwardness.

Another source of irritation to some lesbians is that some of the songs and poetry recited by the entertainers concern having male lovers, and this, to lesbian women, seems unnecessarily repressive in a feminist environment. If the coffeehouse became more lesbian-identified, all women would still be welcome, but entertainment would not contain aspects of intrusive maleness, and lesbians could feel completely relaxed in expressing affection for one another.

Boundary Maintenance

Though Demeter's Daughters has defined itself as a women's space, occasionally men do come in. Sometimes they wander in by accident or out of curiousity. Sometimes they are brought in by their heterosexual partners. In any case, when they come in there is a dilemma, since legally they cannot be refused service, as that might lead to a class action suit.[3]

There was a recent occasion to see how the unwanted intrusion of a man was handled. It was during one of the several birthday parties that are held at the coffeehouse. These celebrations often take place during regular hours—on the weekend or at night—so that women who just wander in are included in the festivities. This evening was a joint birthday for two popular lesbian-feminist professional women who are very active in the community. The two women being honored were surrounded by many of their friends and well-wishers. The place was crowded; the atmosphere was relaxed and full of affection. One of the

---

3. In the last decade, women in the movement have successfully picketed and sued establishments and organizations that have discriminated against them. Now, ironically, that equal-rights laws have made this kind of discrimination illegal, women's businesses have to work out techniques to maintain their own ambience while staying within the law.

9. *A surprise birthday party at the women's coffeehouse.*
(Virginia Morgan)

members of the collective got up and made a short speech wishing the women well. The cakes were cut and passed around to all present, including women who had no direct connection with the celebration.

Unexpectedly, a young man wandered into the building and went quickly into the bookstore, which is not visible from the main room of the coffeehouse. Though there was a volunteer from the coffeehouse sitting in the bookstore, two other women who were part of the regular clientele took the responsibility to join her as she confronted him. She told him quietly that there was a private celebration going on and that he probably would not feel comfortable staying. He protested that he didn't want to hurt anything, but as the two other women came up, he left. The volunteer thanked them for their support, and explained that they had to be very careful since they were not allowed to say directly that it was a women's place and that men were not allowed.

A similar phenomenon occurs in women's bars, but since

125

local gay bars are under the jurisdiction of California State laws, which state that everyone has to be served, and since a primary function of bars is to make a profit, men are present more often. They are usually harmless—too drunk or too unagressive to cause trouble. Sometimes, however, men come into women's bars for voyeuristic purposes, and the women present sense and resent this, and sometimes, partly due to the consumption of alcohol, there is a direct confrontation and physical violence on the part of the women, who resent the presence of curious, prurient men in their territory. Because of the laws, it is often the women who are asked to leave, though the bar has been defined as a lesbian bar. The priority in this case is not to get in trouble with the authorities, whereas with the coffeehouse it is the maintenance of the boundaries of a women's community.

One of the members of the original collective described the function of Demeter's Daughters in the community: "Different groups of women use Demeter's Daughters for different reasons. When we started we saw this as a home for women, a resource center, a place to come to with the literature right here. A place where women can fulfill some of their fantasies. It does that." But most of all, Demeter's Daughters is an environment for feminists in which all of its activities and furnishings reflect and reinforce cultural feminism. By contrast, the Women's Training Center addresses itself to more political, class-oriented needs.

The Women's Training Center

Of the projects that originated in the lesbian-feminist community, the Women's Training Center had some characteristics not shared by others. All seven members of its founding collective were, as one of them described it, "feminists with a lesbian priority," who together had developed a strong class analysis, from which the idea of a Women's Training Center had emerged. Unlike the coffeehouse, which focused on developing and reinforcing a women's culture, the Women's Training Center was more concerned with basic survival. The purpose was to train women in the skills necessary to get jobs heretofore closed to them, and to train them, as well, in techniques of getting such jobs and in agitating politically to encourage companies to change their policies against hiring women in blue-collar skilled trades. The statement of purpose announced to the community:

> We are skilled as auto mechanics, carpenters, electricians, health workers, photographers and teachers.... It is nearly impossible to enter into an apprenticeship without some previous experience in the field, and training opportunities are generally closed to women: what training we have acquired has been primarily from men who don't respect our abilities. We have developed our competence in these skills on our own time and money, finding work opportunities in these fields unavailable to us, and have to earn a living in the traditional positions of typists, file clerks, hospital workers, secretaries and other unskilled laborers.

The statement reflects several things. It is issued by women who have gained knowledge of some of the techniques traditionally relegated to men and have realized that both apprenticeship opportunities and actual jobs are virtually unavailable to women. It addresses itself to the problems of finding jobs with income adequate to support themselves, a situation faced by most lesbians and many single women. Finally, it relates to the feminist view that these blue-collar skills are categorically withheld from women in our culture by men who have the power to do so.

The Women's Training Center developed from a study group of activist women which had formed following a workshop on class analysis at the 1973 Lesbian Conference in Los Angeles. The study group had been meeting locally for several weeks. Some of the members were beginning to feel frustrated because, while they were discussing a range of topics within the perspective of a class analysis, there was no action. To them the analysis, in itself, was not enough.

At that time the women in the study group, which later became the Women's Training Center collective, were all working, but most of them held part-time jobs. They and their friends had been trying to find better jobs and were dissatisfied with the limited jobs available to women. And it seemed to some of them that the local women's community was not addressing itself to the concrete day-to-day economic problems faced by women who have to support themselves. One of the members of the collective describes this:

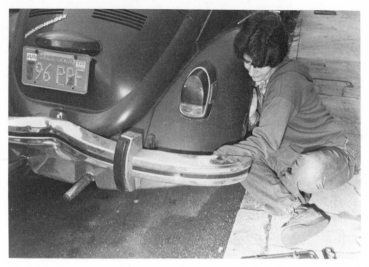

10. Many women in the community are competent mechanics. The Women's Training Center is one place where courses in auto mechanics are taught to women who want these skills. (Virginia Morgan)

It seemed that every single women's organization was focused on the more cultural aspects. We were just so sick and tired of that! I guess we really felt separate from people who had the opportunity or had the privilege to be spending time putting together a coffeehouse.... We wanted to spend the time doing things that could really change our lives. So several of us got together—two of whom were auto mechanics who wanted to put together an auto garage. Out of the study group came a focus of wanting to put together a school where we could put together a lot of skill training. We could get together the women we knew had skills in the community and share the skills with other people. And we could also have other classes— maybe a discussion of lesbians and single women—their lives and how they see themselves politically and changing the world.

The collective decided that the school would be a place exclusively for women, but that the leadership would remain lesbian identified:

We knew if we could make it a place where lesbians felt free and open to be in it, then we knew that there would be other women who would feel free to be open in it. But if it were a place run by straight women, there's a chance that lesbians wouldn't feel free to be in it.

One reason given for the lesbian and single-woman priority was that it is these women who *have* to earn their own living; they cannot depend on other sources of income as other women are sometimes able to do.

While the collective was still talking about developing a women's school, a building became available to them at low cost, and this helped to crystallize the project. The collective members assumed that their venture would become a reality and began to raise money for the Center by using their savings, borrowing from friends, and holding benefits. They realized that the physical nature of the building meant that they could be self-sufficient: they could raise their own money to pay the rent from classes and rent part of the building as a garage run by women.

The members of the collective felt that they wanted to address themselves mainly to two groups of women: those who did not have the skills and wanted to acquire them to upgrade their job potential, and those who had already acquired the skills—usually as a result of being poor and needing to learn to do their own repairs or through growing up in a large family in which these skills were passed on to all the children—but often had no idea how to get a job that would use their skills. There was a third group of women who used the Center, women who were mostly from middle-class backgrounds and had some of the employable skills traditionally held by women, such as secretarial skills, but who wanted to be retrained in the particular skills offered by the Center. Some of these women simply wanted the training so that they could make their own repairs.

The classes were held in eight-week sessions and were announced in catalogues printed at the Center. The teachers were women in the community who were paid a nominal fee by the students to teach them their particular skills. The first classes concentrated on practical skills: plumbing, carpentry, auto and motorcycle repair, and self-defense. The registration sessions included potluck dinners to which the staff and prospective students, as well as any woman in the community who wanted to have dinner with other women, brought homemade food to share. They used the opportunity to meet in small groups with the instructors and to socialize with other women.

It was suggested that the full fee for the course be paid in advance at the registration meeting to protect the instructors, many of whom made their entire living by teaching these classes. However, all courses were given with a sliding fee; for example, streetfighting, the self-defense course, which met three times a week, cost ten dollars a month for women who could afford it; for those who could not, the fee was negotiated. As with other community projects, the policy of the Center was to turn no woman away from a course because she was unable to pay.

Two descriptions of courses, written by their instructors, give an indication of their underlying assumptions that women are an oppressed group and, as such, should learn the skills to fight back against their oppressors.

Streetfighting:
A self-defense course for women using basic Karate techniques and covering real-life situations. Emphasis on dirty fighting. The aim is to prepare women (as well as a short session can) to deal defensively and offensively with violent situations. Classes are disciplined and rigorous with a variety of sparring exercises. Women of all ages and in all states of physical condition are welcome. Every woman can learn to kick ass.

Nor were basic economic survival techniques ignored:

Unemployment Insurance Workshop:
If you're trapped in an oppressive job and need some time and money to find your way out, if you've already been disqualified from receiving unemployment benefits, or if you're receiving them with some hassle; you'd be better off if you knew how the unemployment insurance system works. I'd like to tell you what the laws are and to help you understand the system well enough that you can make them work in your favor. Your employer is periodically trained by people from the unemployment offices on how to keep to a minimum the people collecting from his

account; I feel that employees should get the same advantage.

Because of the streetfighting class, which was widely attended from the beginning, a place in the building had to be fixed up so that barefoot students of karate could use it safely. The rest of the building also needed a lot of work. This necessity set the pattern for the classes, which at first was on-the-job practical experience in fixing the wiring, carpentry, and plumbing in the Center itself. Later, on-the-job experience took place in the homes of community members who needed such jobs done. Women in the community could call the Center and ask that a class be sent out to do repairs. They would pay what they could afford.

This method served two functions: for women who needed the skills, it gave invaluable on-the-job training in real-life situations; women who were on a minimal income and needed repairs done could employ other women at a rate they could afford. In a sense what was created was an ingroup client relationship parallel to the union-dominated system of the majority culture.

As the classes continued and other courses were added— wilderness survival techniques, stained-glass making, improvisational theatre, as well as more courses in basic trade skills—the collective realized that, as the Center was set up, the students did not have the opportunity for enough supervised advanced training in skills to qualify for apprenticeships in the job market. Only a few women teachers were qualified to teach the advanced courses, and even those few were working full time and could teach only one or two nights a week.

Ideally, the Center was intended to fully train women while giving them enough hours to qualify for the requirement to get licenses. However, the collective members realized that with limited funds they could go only one step at a time and provide on-the-job training to women of the community at below-union costs. Despite this, the Center did what it could to further prepare women to get jobs by teaching them how to pass tests and apply for jobs.

The classes stimulated many friendships. For women new in San Francisco, the classes at the Center gave them contact with other women who were likely to share their interests and outlook. The streetfighting class, because it was taught at both a beginning and an increasingly advanced level, was especially conducive to the development of a large network of women, who saw each other three times a week at the class and often met socially outside of class as well. Before and after class, members would talk informally, keeping up with what was happening to each other and in the community. It was assumed that if a woman was a permanent member of the class, she was at least a potential friend.

Most of the regular members of the staff and the classes were lesbian-identified. By affiliating themselves with the Center, they were defined in the larger community of women as politically oriented, working-class feminists who were concerned about the special problems of lesbians and working-class and third-world women rather than the cultural aspects of lesbian-feminism.

One goal of the Center was to get in touch with third-world and other working-class women who had not participated in community activities because they either were unaware of them or felt that these were not addressed to their particular needs. One of the collective members explained in a taped interview how they first made contact with some of these women:

> We [the Women's Training Center collective and a third-world politically oriented lesbian group] came together on a lot of issues around class and race. We're really an organization that is doing something that relates directly to class, work, and money. And they're doing something that relates directly to racism. So we could easily come together and support each other. So that started it.
>
> Q: How did you get in touch with each other? How did they find out about you?
>
> A: Socially. Absolutely. I guess it was just through the grapevine. And their group was forming when the Center was forming. And we knew certain people in each other's organizations. And lovers—

When the third-world group became the local steering committee to raise money for the defense of a black woman prisoner, they asked members of the Center collective to help. The two groups together planned the program for a benefit, which was given at the Center and which raised money for the cause and succeeded in bringing together members of the community who had heretofore felt that they had little in common. In reciprocation, subsequent benefits were held jointly by both groups to raise money for expenses incurred at the Center.

Soon after this, structural changes took place which significantly affected the development of the Center. The members of the collective who had held part-time jobs to support themselves so they could keep the Center running, all got full-time jobs. As with other volunteer-run projects, this meant they no longer were able to give first priority to running the Center themselves. When a small grant from a feminist organization came through to permit the hiring of someone to coordinate the Center's programs, the collective met to discuss what direction they felt the project should take. Some of the women wanted a more lesbian-separatist orientation, while the majority felt they should involve more third-world and working-class women in the leadership of the Center. They decided collectively to use the money from the grant to hire a third-world woman so that new ideas would be generated from which programs might develop.

However, as one member of the collective pointed out, it was difficult to deal with the inherent racist implications of a collective of white former volunteers who became employers of one black woman. The woman had been hired to stay in the office in the Center, answer the telephone, and come up with programs. But she felt that her working conditions were cold and lonely, and after a while she stopped coming so often. The situation became critical when the landlady threatened to cancel the lease because she had been promised that someone would be in the building regularly.

By this time only three members of the original collective were still involved in running the Center. They met to decide what to do about the problem and came up with the solution of voting the collective out of existence and evaluating where they would be then. The collective no longer needed to hold on to the position of leadership; they had gone as far as they could in laying the groundwork, opening the Center, offering the classes, and bringing in people. As one of them said in an interview:

133

We have a crisis where there are third world women who aren't getting what they want, who are dissatisfied, who have needs that we cannot meet, but who are here. We have a woman who is teaching classes, and who has a lot to lose if this place closes down. We have a printing project that is just beginning. . . . We are now looking at the Center for what actually happens there. Forget about the dreams, forget looking at the future, we know we can only go so far. . . . So we faced the fact that there are four women here whose livelihood depends on having access to this building. . . . We decided to have the teachers be responsible for their classes and the woman who does the printing project could print up the bulletins. It doesn't need volunteers to do it. It became real important to a number of us to get rid of the volunteer-type organization. . . . We know that women's organizations are not going to have power and are not going to go on unless women are making their living, and having a first priority doing that project.

The collective was dissolved, and the actual running of the Center was turned over to the third-world employee and the teachers, who ran it as a team. All of them had a personal investment in making the Center work. As a member of the founding collective summed it up:

There are a bunch of third-world women who could use a place where they have the leadership. . . . What I'm hoping is going to happen is that not only the women who are there in the building, but other women who have not had access to a building, to money, to the kind of thing that went on in the Center can now take over these resources and turn them over to themselves.

This was done, with some of the members of the original collective making themselves available as technical advisors, since they had expertise in raising money and other skills that were not widely shared by the new organizers.

The careers of Demeter's Daughters and the Women's Training Center show how the interests and backgrounds of the women involved influenced the nature and development of the projects. Demeter's Daughters, a more middle-class and culturally focused enterprise, survived a deep split and remained intact and in the hands of the founding collective responsible for it. The Women's Training Center, more specifically political and working-class in orientation, was transformed and turned over to the clientele it was designed to serve; this development, too, was in keeping with its underlying ideology.

5.   LESBIAN MOTHERS

Lesbian mothers are important to an understanding of the lesbian-feminist community for two reasons: as a group they are the members of the community most persecuted by outsiders; and because they are mothers, their child-care practices lend insight into how community values are defined and transmitted.

The social role of the lesbian mother is an emerging one, of which little has been written. The lesbian mother is in a marginal position in two communities. To heterosexuals, because she is a lesbian, she is generally considered to be a negative influence on her own children: it is assumed that she will socialize them to be homosexual. To members of the lesbian community she is in an ambiguous position: because of her association with the father of her children, they are not certain that she is a "real" lesbian. And many of her needs as a mother are unmet in the lesbian community, since most of the community activities are directed toward women without children. In defense of their marginal position, lesbian mothers have recently banded together in self-help groups. They are concerned about working out a viable lifestyle for themselves and their children, establishing support networks, and actively combating the social and legal discrimination they face.

There are two categories of lesbian mothers—those who have had children within the framework of a heterosexual marriage and those who have not. The experience of lesbians who are mothers in coming to terms with their lesbianism is similar to

136

that of lesbians who are not, but for them it is complicated by other factors.

Married Lesbian Mothers

Because lesbians have been socialized as heterosexual women in our culture and have been raised to share the common expectation of marrying a man, married lesbian mothers often come to a realization of their lesbian identitiy in different stages, somewhat analogous to the coming out process described on p. 34. Some women are aware that they are lesbians before they get married, but they hope that a heterosexual marriage will "cure" them of what the popularization of Freudian thought has taught them is an arrested stage of sexual and emotional development. After they have had children, some of these women find that the strain of living in a way that is artificial for them is ultimately too damaging. They come to terms with their lesbianism, leave the marriage, and with their children try to find a new life that they can lead more honestly.

Other women come to a realization of their lesbianism only after they have been married and had children. Sometimes they find, often to their own surprise, that they have fallen in love with another woman. Yet, the decision to leave one's husband is difficult to make. All of one's social expectations are against such a move. As with most divorced women, the level of income drops sharply. Then, too, it sometimes takes a while to adjust to a new social role, especially one thought by some of the women concerned to be in conflict with the role of mother.

Certainly a large part of the decision to leave a marriage and live as a lesbian mother concerns what is best for the children. Many women, though willing to carry on a lesbian affair, will not leave a heterosexual marriage, because they feel that to do so will be harmful for their children. Such women hesitate to identify themselves as lesbians; rather, they are inclined to feel, as do some newly emerging lesbians who are unmarried, that the affair in which they find themselves is a special one between two people who love each other, but that it will not be repeated. Such "special" relationships can last for years, and the heterosexual marriage is maintained as well. In recent years, however, with the spread of feminist politics and the emergence of lesbian-feminist self-help organizations, many such women, who traditionally would have stayed married, do leave their husbands and move with their children and a partner into the lesbian community.

Unmarried Lesbian Mothers

There are two ways for unmarried lesbians to acquire children: through adoption and by deliberately becoming pregnant. Women who do not themselves want to give birth but want to raise children often try to adopt them. Adoption agencies have increasingly allowed single women and men to adopt the more difficult-to-place older or handicapped children, although the agencies continue to prefer married couples. Women who want to adopt children through recognized agencies do not make an issue of their lesbianism, since most agencies consider homosexuality undesirable in a potential parent. In the local lesbian community, however, most women have not adopted children through an agency; rather, they raise children without formally adopting them, because they have been asked to do so by the mother. In such cases, the new mother is conscientious about her responsibility and turns to other women in the community for advice and support.

Lesbians who do not want to get married but want the experience of giving birth to their own children, consider the decision carefully. They are very concerned about the kind of man who will be the biological father. It is widely held in the community that homosexual men make the best candidates, since current folklore is that they are "biologically" more likely to produce nonsexist children. It is also felt that they are less likely to make demands on the mother or the children after birth; that they can enjoy a friendly relationship if the circumstances allow, without the need to establish a "property" relationship with their children, a need said to be more characteristic of heterosexual men.

Many women who are not mothers when they enter the community plan to have children or acquire children afterward. They may want to do this to enhance an especially good long-term relationship, or a particular woman may want the experience of caring for her own child. One couple, who have been together for several years, discussed with me the possibility of their having children. Both are in their late twenties and are in the long process of professional training; when they have finished, they want to raise a child together. They feel that by then they will be old enough and secure enough economically to care for a child properly. They decided that the older of the two was entitled to get pregnant first, although either is willing if need be. They are aware that there are many aspects of this project to be worked out. They talked with me about some of these: the decision of who should be the father, what any kind of emotional relationship with a man would imply, and the nature of the man's subsequent interaction with the child, the mother, and the mother's partner.

During the period of fieldwork, several women talked about getting pregnant, but to my knowledge none of these women have actually done so. There are various reasons for delay. First, the momentum of daily life and its problems make it easy to put off an act that would dramatically change the life of the woman. Second, the lives of many of the women are characterized by change—of job, of residence, of living group—and that to commit oneself to the momentous undertaking of having a baby without long-term and consistent support seems overwhelming. Finally, many women who want children are so deeply committed to separatism that they cannot bring themselves to have a child in common with a man. Therefore, they look with interest on developments in the techniques of cloning and parthenogenesis. By using these artificial methods of creating children, the need to have contact with men is alleviated. However, as yet, these techniques are not immediately available.

Legal Situation

The biggest threat to most lesbian mothers is a legal one. In child custody cases that are contested, the very fact of the mother's lesbianism is usually enough for the judge to decide that she is unfit, regardless of other qualities she may possess. If the lesbianism is hidden and custody is granted, should the lesbianism be discovered later, the children's father, or even another, more distant relation, may be successful in contesting the mother's right to raise her children. As one of the founders of the Seattle-based Lesbian Mothers' National Defense Fund explained:

All lesbian mothers live with the omnipresent fear that somebody's going to take the kids away. The fear is always there. No matter how secure things may seem, there's always the chance that the father, the father's parents, the mother's parents, or the state might try to get the kids. *Advocate*, October 22, 1975 p. 34)

The children's father and other relatives are not the only threats to the lesbian mother's custody rights. In the case of women on marginal incomes, for example, representatives of a social agency, social workers, schoolteachers, welfare case workers, doctors or other employees of health care clinics— who tend to share conventional values about how to raise children—may bring a custody suit against unconventional family situations. For a detailed account of a lesbian mother's fight to keep custody of her son, see Gibson (1977); for a more narrowly legal reference, see Basile (1974). Mothers in such cases are beginning to have some recourse. Community members are quick to hold demonstrations in their support; women's centers, lesbian associations, lesbian mothers' groups, local legal-aid programs, and civil liberties unions all are likely to have lists of local lawyers who are willing to take these cases on principle.

When such cases involve lesbian charges, two sources of authoritative help have recently become available for use in court. The first is a resolution by the American Psychiatric Association, which declared in 1973 that homosexuality is no longer considered a pathology. This resolution now makes possible expert testimony by members of the psychiatric profession in support of lesbian-mothered families.

The second is the use of two educational films, *Sandy and Madeleine's Family* (1973) and *In the Best Interests of the Children* (1977). The first was made for use in court in the case of the two lesbian mothers in the film who were lovers. Their case was the first in which known lesbians ultimately got unconditional custody of their children, after several appeals.[1] The

1. The original citations for these cases are Isaacson V. Isaacson, No. D-36867 (Washington Superior Court, King County, September 3, 1973), and Schuster V. Schuster, No. D-36868, Washington Superior Court, King County, September 3, 1974. My thanks to Joan Girard at the University of California Law Library at Boalt Hall in Berkeley for her help in finding these citations.

11. Lesbian and heterosexual supporters and their children demonstrate for the right of lesbian mothers to maintain custody of their children. (Copyright: Chronicle Publishing Co., 1977)

141

movie features scenes from their family life and testimonies of support from a variety of professionals involved in the case. The second is about eight lesbian mothers and their children and includes a group discussion of children of lesbian mothers and professional workers who are knowledgeable about lesbian mothers. Both films, by showing actual interaction and attitudes of the mothers, attempt to break down stereotypes of lesbian mothers as somehow different from heterosexual mothers in quality of care and concern about their children. Though both films are excellent for educational purposes, it is up to the discretion of the judge in each case whether the movies are admissable in court.

Despite the films and the APA resolution, the best advice for lesbian mothers is to avoid court battles over custody if at all possible; the chance that a known lesbian mother will retain custody of her children is still meager, and it is estimated that a contested custody case involving a lesbian mother costs at least $10,000 for lawyer fees by the time it reaches the appeals court. These cases may also drag on for several years (*Advocate*, October 22, 1975, p. 25).

Lesbian Mothers' Self-help Groups

Because of the legal persecution and the social isolation that lesbian mothers face, the realization that they need support groups has resulted in one of the most innovative organizations that has sprung up in the lesbian community, the Lesbian Mothers' Union (now Lesbian Mothers and Friends).

As with the founding of the Daughters of Bilitis in 1955, it is significant that a second, equally precedent-breaking lesbian organization, the Lesbian Mothers' Union, also coalesced in San Francisco. Over the years, the local Daughters of Bilitis members had included lesbian mothers. Membership in the organization had helped lesbian mothers realize they were not alone. The organization periodically arranged discussion sessions to help them cope with their situation. Yet, as the membership changed, the focus of the organization shifted as well. As the proportion of active members who were in their twenties and without children increased, the concerns of lesbian mothers tended to be overlooked.

Furthermore, the advent of feminist awareness helped to

create a new population of lesbian mothers in San Francisco, who did not join the Daughters of Bilitis. Most lesbian mothers were still isolated from each other; they more closely identified themselves as part of the general lesbian community, although many of their needs differed from those of the more socially active members with no children. It was not until local lesbian mothers attended the West Coast Gay Women's Conference in Los Angeles in 1971 that the Lesbian Mothers' Union was formed. One of its more active members, in an interview, describes its inception:

At a lesbian conference in L.A. no arrangements had been made for child-care . . . and the assumption was made that lesbians don't have children. And this assumption was made by gay women, who obviously were not in touch with gay women. [Del Martin appeared on a panel and remarked that neither the gay nor the women's movement addressed the problems of lesbian mothers] at which point a woman got up and said: "I am a lesbian and I have two children. And no arrangements have been made for me at all. If I had not had a place for my children to stay, I would not have been able to come here." That very day a workshop was set up for lesbian mothers. That was *the first time ever since Sappho* that lesbianism mixed with motherhood had been talked about. [In fact, the Daughters of Bilitis had held discussions about lesbian motherhood but few women now in the community knew about them.]

A month later [July 1971], a meeting was called in Oakland, using names of women who had been at the Los Angeles workshop who lived in the area. There was a good response, and out of this, the Lesbian Mothers' Union was formed, which soon moved to San Francisco.

It took several months and several different turns of what people needed to be talked about at lesbian mothers' meetings. It included how to tell your lover you have babies, how to tell your lover if you want children, what to do if you're living in a household with children, how you relate to those children, how do other people relate to them, should we, in fact, start working to get lobbyists to work for repeal of the unfit mother law—because it is not a written law that because you're a lesbian you should have your children taken away—it is an assumption made by all judges, or has been. . . .

At any rate, out of that grew what happened twice last year and that was that two couples, one in California and one in Washington [state] gained custody of their children for the first time [as admitted lesbians] in the history of the world so far as we know, and I don't believe that that would have happened unless we had a Lesbian Mothers' Union to at least let other people know that lesbian mothers did exist. So it has been through that that the lesbian mothers' "liberation" movement has actually started and has gotten as far as it has. There are chapters springing up all over the country.

At first the group was described by one of its more active members as a "crisis hot line," in that most members did not meet regularly; but when a problem arose, such as a threatened custody suit, members would be telephoned and would rally to help.

Gradually the group expanded and began to hold regular meetings and more frequent social and fund-raising events. The focus shifted from group discussions to more direct political action. By May 1975 part of the membership decided to split off and broaden the membership base by allowing interested feminists who were not lesbian mothers to join. At this point, the group that split off became Lesbian Mothers and Friends, while the members who were left became gradually less active. With the addition of new members to the new group, more activities could be carried out. The expanded group began to meet regularly twice a month.

The San Francisco lesbian mothers' group is the first of similar autonomous groups to be established throughout the country. There is communication among the groups about common problems and activities. Some of them have focused on issues of special importance to their particular community. For example, the Lesbian Mothers' National Defense Fund—in Seattle, where Sandy and Madeleine's case (about which the movie was made) was decided—has focused on the legal aspects of lesbian-mother cases and has built up a body of legal precedents to help other such cases wherever they may be tried. The local

San Francisco group had arranged for lesbian law students to compile a collection of legal precedents, now on file with the Women's Litigation Unit of the San Francisco Neighborhood Legal Assistance Foundation, that have special relevance in California courts. There is still a need for responsible research on the effects on the children who live in a lesbian-headed household. Some lesbian mothers have consulted with child-care professionals and family service agencies about legitimizing their family style. These active lesbian mothers' groups have made the lesbian family visible as a viable family unit, and through the efforts of their members in tackling the legal and family service professions, they have succeeded in altering many assumptions that previously caused arbitrary breakups of successful family groups.

The San Francisco Lesbian Mothers and Friends estimates that it has about 130 members. It is thought that there are several times that number of lesbian mothers in the area who do not know about the group or with whom it is not in touch. Many of the women who most need the support of the group do not attend its meetings. Single mothers, who are the sole source of care for their children, are often simply too tired in the evenings to go to meetings. Others, on marginal incomes, cannot afford even the two hours of babysitting that attending meetings entails. Some feel that they are too vulnerable to expose themselves as lesbian mothers, even to a group of women in a similar situation. Yet, there is a strong need to meet with other sympathetic women who share the same problems, within a similar lesbian-feminist framework. For example, a notice on a bulletin board at the women's coffeehouse said: "Lesbian Mothers. Where are you? *I need you!* Call ——."

Lesbian Mothers and Friends regularly holds social and fund-raising events in which the entire family can participate; one of the purposes of these events is to encourage children of lesbian mothers to meet other children who share the same family background, to counteract any sense of being different that the children may experience from schoolmates. Sometimes, if women are unable to attend meetings regularly, they do manage to attend the social events with their children.

A basic concern of the lesbian mothers who were interviewed is raising children in a nonsexist environment, one in which both the children and the parent have love and support, plus the freedom to develop in whatever ways are important to them. In keeping with the values of the community at large, both a mutual support system and the encouragement of independence and growth are stressed. To meet these needs, it is necessary to develop a substitute extended-kin system among affectionate and concerned adults who care about the children. Lesbian mothers also want financial security for their family and protection from outside divisive forces. Most of them favor alternative forms of education so that their own influence on their children is not daily contradicted by the orientation and methods of the public schools, which they feel squelch individuality and imagination. Most lesbian mothers are concerned, as well, about working out good relationships with their children and their partners. In this process, they try to maintain a sense of their own needs as they try to be responsive to the needs of those for whom they are responsible.

Many lesbian mothers are working to build a growing set of legal data so that any lawyer defending a lesbian mother has access to such material. As more data are available about the nature of lesbian-mothered families and the effect on children growing up in such homes, it is hoped that the specious argument that lesbian mothers are "unfit" will become as archaic as other such prejudices.

Lesbian mothers who have banded together in the Lesbian Mothers and Friends have actively worked to change their situation. Through the organization they have established support and friendship networks on which they can draw for familial social life, for advice from others who have successfully contended with their mutual problems, and for help when needed. Lesbian Mothers and Friends has often rallied to the cause when a mother faces a custody case, in helping to find a sympathetic lawyer, in supporting women and children going through this ordeal, and in helping to establish the family or to continue the fight if the case has been decided against the woman.

At a meeting of Lesbian Mothers and Friends in December 1975, some of these issues were raised. A detailed description of the meeting is useful in showing the nature of the issues and how the group responded to them. As with all such meetings, the women sat in a circle. Each woman gave her first name only and added whatever information she wanted to about herself; no one was urged to say more than she had volunteered, the assumption being that some women would be in particularly vulnerable positions if it were known that they had attended meetings of the organization. After the meeting, some of the women stayed to talk with other women, to arrange to get together with their families during the week and thus expand their personal networks.

A woman with a baby spoke about her situation; she was still living with her husband though he knew she was a lesbian. She wanted to leave him and live in the community, but felt she had to find out more about what that entailed before actually making the break. Some of the members made arrangements to help her find a place to live and to set up child-care if she wants it.

Another woman came with her partner. The mother had been ill, and because of this, her teen-age daughter had been placed in a foster home temporarily. Both women were afraid that the social worker assigned to their case was trying to arrange for the mother to be declared unfit so that the foster parents could adopt the child. Apparently, since the birthrate has fallen in this country, there are fewer children available for legitimate adoption, while the demand for children has grown. Many mothers who are on welfare programs believe that some of the professional workers attached to these programs are on the alert to find reasons to take their children away from them so that they can be placed in more conventional families who want to adopt them. There are no available data to support this anxiety, but it is a real fear of the mothers concerned. Some of the women in the room had been in similar situations, and they counseled the two women about possible solutions.

Another woman had come to the area to establish a home for her child while she left the child with friends. She had moved into a mixed commune with people she trusted, and she thought she could properly care for her child there. After she described her situation, the other women discussed what she would need to carry out her plan. They decided to pay for two return plane tickets, out of the limited funds the group had raised. They assumed that the mother could get to her destination by herself, probably by hitchhiking, but felt that the child should not have to face the uncertainties of either hitchhiking with the mother or flying alone. This decision was made by consensus. The woman had not asked for money; the group simply felt from their knowledge of children in unpredictable situations that this would be the best solution for the child.

The subject of another emerging social group, gay fathers, was raised. Such men rarely have the opportunity of living with their children; however, a few homosexual fathers, inspired by the example of the lesbian mothers' groups, wanted to be allowed to join the group to discuss problems they had in common. It was up to the women present to decide what to do, and they all were asked to address themselves to the problem. One woman said that she didn't want to spend so much time on it, but another woman explained that it was important to find out how each one felt so that future policies could take these differences into account when decisions were required. After a period of discussion—in which it was pointed out that the participation of gay men in the group would alter the nature of its interaction and that once again women would be giving their energies to men instead of working on their own problems—it was decided that some of the women would help men start their own group.[2]

Finally a report was made which summarized the current situation of the organization. One of the gains made since the group was started in 1971 was that many of the children of the members were getting to know each other and to play together. Several group activities centering around holidays had taken place or were being planned regularly. One of these is an annual Christmas party, sponsored by local gay men's organizations for lesbian mothers and their children. The report included information about alternative educational facilities. The women were concerned that the facilities would not be too expensive, that the children would receive a good education, and that the policy of the staff would be sensitive to the values of the family.

Lesbian mothers were also reported as able to consult with various social service and mental health agencies. Martin and Lyon had described the activities of the lesbian mother's group

2. By 1977 there was an active gay fathers group with an estimated sixty members. Some of these men lived with their wives as well as their children. Others had or wanted part-time custody.

as early as 1972:

> The Lesbian Mothers Union is working cooperatively
> with San Francisco's Family Service Agency to develop a
> program which would include a redefinition of what consti-
> tutes a family, confrontation between lesbian mothers and
> the agency's counseling staff to assess the agency's clinical
> approaches to families headed by lesbians, a research
> study to evaluate the quality of care and home life of the
> children of lesbians, legal aid in obtaining expert witnesses
> for contested custody hearings involving lesbian mothers,
> and a mass media campaign to educate the public about
> the realities of the lesbian life style. (P. 161)

Some common problems were also mentioned in the report at
the meeting. One is that lesbians without children sometimes
isolate lesbian mothers, or ask them to care for children at all-
gay events. In either case, the lesbian mother is being stereotyped by members of her own community. There are, as well,
common problems concerning children: with partners or lovers,
with ex-husbands, with relatives, with the courts, with an
inadequate income.

Many of these are recurrent problems that are related to the
structure of society. Others are problems that all single parents
face; some are specific to lesbian mothers alone. The addition of
the lesbian mothers' organization to the community goes a long
way in providing the crucial elements—information, a support
group, and a commitment to activism to change an untenable
situation—to resolve some of these problems.

Two ongoing expenses for lesbian mothers are legal costs and
living expenses. It is not unusual for a lesbian mother suddenly
to find herself facing a court battle for custody of her children.
The lesbian mothers' organization tries to have a large enough
balance in its treasury so that the expenses for these emergencies can be underwritten or at least somewhat alleviated. Members of the group also undertake to help families on marginal
incomes during emergencies. For example, one mother of five
children had her welfare check stolen. Other lesbian mothers
immediately contributed to the living expenses of her family
though they themselves were on marginal incomes.

149

Because of these expenses, the lesbian mothers' group depends on the larger lesbian community to participate in its fund-raising events. The best known of these is the annual Mother's Day Auction held at a lesbian bar, in which members of the community contribute and bid for goods and services to benefit the lesbian mothers. More than two hundred women attend these auctions, and the bidding is lively. Lesbian Mothers and Friends also sponsors benefit dances for women, which are widely attended. Through publicity and by means of these fund-raising events, most members of the lesbian community have become aware of and are strong supporters of lesbian mothers, and the lesbian mother has become more integrated into the general lesbian community.

Lesbian Mothers and Their Children

In the process of accepting one's lesbianism, other kinds of social relationships are being reexamined. For example, many lesbian mothers are reassessing the adult-child, sexually specific role assignments usually considered the norm in heterosexual nuclear families. Both in the public press and in interviews on which this study is based, there is frequent criticism of family relations in our society and a vision of change to which lesbian mothers, as well as feminists generally, feel themselves committed. Jill Johnston, a well-known lesbian-feminist, writing in *Ms* magazine in 1972, makes the following critique:

> The end of motherhood (and of course, fatherhood) means the end to parent chauvinism and child oppression, an end to private property and authoritative representation. Women already are standing up and saying that being a mother in a ticky-tacky box looking after her possessions is an abnormal unhealthy situation.... We may be the *instruments* of creation, but we have no right to own and dominate our products after we provide the nourishment of the abjectly dependent stage. That no woman can become herself in service to dependents for whom she is the sole source of guidance and well-being. That women like men have become slaves to the fabrication of parental superiority.... And all the other interrelated reasons for terminating the source unit of large-scale worldwide op-

pression by class, race, age, and sex; the modern patriarchal nuclear family. As I see it, the movement for childcare centers is an important transitional measure on the way back to the large communal families of multiple parents. Such families exist in the hippie commune form and they remain oppressive to women. *Possibly the only "liberated" communal families at this time are the lesbian mother households*—the total child-care center. A cooperative community of little adults and big children merging identities and responsibilities and exchanging skills and information in an atmosphere of consciousness and mutual respect. (P. 124)

A vision of a better mode of family life is implied by a statement written by a group of lesbian mothers who discussed their feelings and perceptions for a self-help book for feminists.

Lesbian mothers have to keep in mind that we are building something, but we're not quite sure what it will look like when we're done. We know it's an alternative to the present family structure and the present male-female role models. It's nothing less than an alternative to sexism....

We know it is a society where people are free to love whom they choose, openly and honestly, without having to lie or apologize. It's a society where women are respected and children are nobody's burden, everybody's responsibility. A society in which "family" means people, children and adults who have made a commitment to one another, who will support each other emotionally, financially, and spiritually. A society in which children are encouraged to develop all their interests and explore all the possibilities for living rather than be channeled into a narrow mold depending on sex, class or race.

If those who have more comfortable, traditional lives tell us that this is utopia, we must admit that it is. "But," we tell them, "we have no place else to live." The world we inherited does not have room for us; it has smothered and crazed many already, and our children cannot grow up here without being twisted and distorted. So we must build, with all those who are willing to help, a new home

151

for ourselves, our friends, and our children. We cannot rest here, content with the present. We must, like children, live at the edge of tomorrow. (Women in Transition, Inc., 1975, pp. 86–87)

These attitudes are reflected in ways in which lesbian mothers confront their day-to-day problems, which are made complicated by the fact that they are and feel themselves to be a minority of stigmatized people in a larger culture. From the interviews and observations, it is apparent that lesbian-feminist mothers believe themselves to be in a transitional stage, in which they try to live their lives and raise their children in terms of nonhierarchical principles. Because, as they put it, they themselves were raised in a sexist culture, they feel they must overcome the results of this early training. Their children are surrounded by aspects of a culture that they are trying to change, and they find it difficult to get reinforcement for these values outside of the small lesbian or feminist groups in which they move. Their hope is that their children, raised in a nonsexist environment, will be able to live lives closer to the ideal.

The mothers in the study frequently expressed the hope that their children would feel free to show their feelings and to give and receive affection and approval. They link this desire with memories of their own experiences while growing, especially if during adolescence they became aware of their lesbianism and were forced to suppress it. Many women report being raised by parents who felt it was wrong to show too much affection. The scars of these emotional dishonesties linger, and they are determined that their own children will not be so deprived. They do their best to show affection readily, to listen attentively to how their children feel, and to take these feelings into consideration in their actions. They want their daughters and sons to allow themselves to be tender and nurturing, strong and self-confident, without regard to their sex. They want their children to allow themselves the full range of emotion available to them—to be, in fact, the "first generation of human beings."

Lesbian Mothers as a Minority

It cannot be overly stressed how intrusive the various aspects of concealment and reaction to it are in the lives of lesbians

12. *A lesbian mother and her children at her son's birthday party. This mother is fighting for custody of her children. (Cathy Cade)*

raising their children. In literature about immigrants, it has been pointed out how, though the world at large was a potentially dangerous and hostile place, the home and small community were sources of support and places to learn how to survive as members of a stigmatized minority group (Howe, 1976, p. 172). Similarly, children of lesbian mothers, especially those living with other lesbian women, have to be taught early to be guarded about the nature of their home environment until they can learn to trust the person to whom they are relating. If the affectional preference of the mother becomes known to the wrong people, the results can be retribution against the mother because of her orientation, ostracism of the child by peers and adults, and ultimately the most threatening, removal of the child from the influence of its mother by the father, by local court order, by misinformed but concerned relatives.

To counteract the negative views of their lifestyle held by some members of the larger culture, most lesbian mothers try to instill in their children a necessary sense of distance in the hope that the children will not develop negative judgments about themselves and their families. The mothers also try to give the children positive reinforcement by socializing with other lesbian mothers and their children, and by allowing their children contact with other people who do not share these negative views. Like other concerned minority parents, they try to be especially loving and supportive to the children within the bounds of the family circle as well, so that, as one lesbian mother put it, "our home is a kind of haven from the ugliness of the outside world."

Explaining to the Children

A divorced lesbian mother is faced with the task of informing the children about her lesbianism and its implications for them as a family. One woman, a mother of two boys and two girls, described to me how she explained to her children about the shift in their lifestyle. She had kept quiet about her lesbian feelings on the advice of her lawyer until her divorce was final. After the divorce, she came to San Francisco to get settled and then sent for the children.

> When they got here I explained what lesbianism was, what my lesbianism meant as I related to them. To each child I had to explain it differently because of the age groups. I can't remember exactly how I explained it to my thirteen-year-old son, but I said that my definition of a lesbian is a woman who is emotionally, psychologically, physically, *committed* to another woman or other women. And usually it is that I have a preference for women. It means that I prefer to be with women rather than with men. So it gets broken down because the children ask me questions and then we have to go through this whole thing.
>
> Q: Doesn't he think you're rejecting him because he's a male?
>
> A: Not anymore. When it was first discussed, his immediate reaction was that I didn't like him because he is a male. And that took more than just one time of my reassuring him that I am his mother and I don't relate to my children in the same way that I relate to anyone else, so that had to be understood, too.

Another mother explained that it took time for the children to understand. After all, she said: "They don't get up one morning and say: 'Hey mom, how come you're gay today?' "

Sometimes children may decide to live with the father for awhile because the implications of a new lifestyle are too threatening. Most children in the community, however, are finally able to accept the change for themselves and for their families, but are still concerned about the opinions of outsiders. Several mothers have mentioned that when they are affectionate with their lovers in public, their children will ask them not to be so demonstrative, explaining: "I understand but the neighbors won't."

Relations with the Children's Father

Not surprisingly, the shift from middle-class, capitalist, heterosexual attitudes to lesbian-feminist and sometimes lesbian-feminist-socialist attitudes leads to complications in child raising. The mix of conflicting ideology and emotion can put a tremendous strain on the children and their parents. The situation is made even more complicated because in any serious disagreement between the father and the lesbian mother, the father has the weight of both society and the courts behind him. There is always the implicit threat that if the mother doesn't do what he wants, the children can be taken away from her.

Conflicts between fathers and lesbian mothers in relationship to their children are of various sorts. The simplest and most disturbing occurs when the ex-husband does not know that the mother is a lesbian. Often, lesbian mothers have to make the decision to teach their children "situational ethics"—to act one way in one context and another in other social situations. If the father does not know that the mother is a lesbian—a concealment easier to maintain if they live in different areas—she sees to it that he does not find out, though this goes against her principles of being open about her lifestyle, especially with her children.

Many informants who tend to see men as interested chiefly in material advantages and indifferent or insensitive to emotion, try not to denigrate their ex-husbands, since the children have loyalty to both parents. Some of these mothers say that they explain to the children that their father does things his way, and that when the children are with their fathers they should decide if what the father wants to do is right for them then. In their mother's home. things are done differently.

155

Other mothers, convinced that the influence of the ex-husbands on the children will be too harmful, simply refuse to allow them access to the children if they are in a position to do so. Then, too, some ex-husbands choose not to have further contact with their children after the divorce. A few fathers have even won custody in court and then, after trying to take full-time care of the children, find it too difficult and send them to their mother to raise. As a lawyer explained: "They just want to win."

Mothers Who Give Up Their Children

Although almost all lesbian mothers want to care for their children and fight, often against great odds, to do so, some feminists—both lesbian and nonlesbian—are reassessing the cultural expectations of biological motherhood. One lesbian (with no children) recently questioned (in an interview) even the most basic aspect of parenthood:

> There is a lot of stuff being done on motherhood now. Who the hell is the biological mother? Some women can carry a child and can't conceive it, and some can conceive but not carry. And it's getting to the place where it might be possible for one woman to be inseminated, another to carry the child, still a third to nurse it and a fourth to bring it up. *Who* is the mother? I think we've made a real fetish of motherhood.

Some women who are ideologically committed to separatism say that they will take the responsibility for raising a girl child, but will relinquish the care of a boy to an appropriate male adult to bring up. An "appropriate male adult" is not necessarily the child's biological father, it should be said; rather, if the mother has any choice, it is a man who is self-conscious about his own sexist tendencies and is in the process of trying to overcome them. These sexist tendencies, or tendencies toward the acquisition of power, are felt by these women to be inherent in any male raised in our culture prior to the advent of feminism, when sexist assumptions first began to be rigorously questioned.

In practice, to my knowledge, few women actually turn over their male children to these men to bring up; however, they do make attempts to be sure that nonsexist men are frequently in contact with their children, perhaps as members of their communes. Jill Johnston, in a speech, reported that she had arranged for her twelve-year-old son to move into a collective of men who had developed a Men's Liberation group and were dedicated to working through incipient sexism in their own lives.

The practice of keeping female children and turning males over to be raised elsewhere has precedent in how the Amazons were thought to live. The progeny that followed from ritual coupling were divided by sex, the girls to be raised by their mothers as warriors, the boys to be turned over to the tribe their fathers belonged to. In this way, the continuity of the tribe was assured, while intimate contact with men was kept to a minimum (Graves, 1966, p. 127; Johnston, 1972, p. 90). Part of a mother's reluctance to raise a son seems to be based on a theory of innate dominance of the male, that any person with a penis is imbued from birth with a sense of his superiority over all females, no matter what his upbringing. A few women feel that if they had a son they would give him up, simply because they would not want to be intimidated by "the enemy" in their own homes.

In addition to such ideologically modified behavior, one must take into account the effect on lesbian mothers of a general shift in our society toward a redefinition of parental responsibility. The shibboleth that a mother's first responsibility is to her children is being reexamined. It has been pointed out by some feminists that men have the prerogative to give up child custody because of career pressures and that women do not. The assumptions underlying this attitude still need to be reassessed in light of the actual number of working mothers and the differing expectations about women's lives.

Sometimes mothers give up custody of their children if they feel that they are unable to give them proper care, either because they lack the money or because the mother's situation is such that the full-time burdens of child-raising are too heavy a drain on her as a single parent. Thus, both the overworked mother and the children who are dependent on her will suffer.

In both cases—that in which mothers prefer not to have the responsibility of raising their sons for ideological reasons, and that in which women choose alternatives to full-time custody of children of either sex—the assumption that the mother is automatically the best person to have full-time child-care responsibilities is gradually being altered in light of the needs of both the children and the parents.

Despite all of these ideological considerations, mothers who give up custody in favor of part-time visiting rights are somewhat stigmatized and are considered "unnatural" by much of the majority culture and by some lesbians who, though ideologically in accord with this decision, identify to some extent with the children who are being given up. This area is one of the most emotionally laden in the shifts in role expectations.

Living Arrangements

Most lesbian mothers who were interviewed are on an economic subsistence level. Some are living on alimony or child support payments from their former husbands or both; many are in the welfare program Aid to Dependent Children. Some lesbian mothers have part-time jobs, either as their only source of income or as a supplement to other sources. Most lesbian mothers, except those few who work full-time at professional jobs, have to contend with insufficient financial income.

The combination of a minimum income and the desire to surround their children with other adults and children influences the living arrangements that many lesbian mothers make. Because they are usually too poor to afford to rent or buy adequate housing for themselves and their children, lesbian mothers usually live with other adults who share the lesbian-feminist priorities of the family. Some others simply exchange room and board for baby-sitting. Others form partnerships in which the rent, expenses, and child-care responsibilities are shared if possible.

Sometimes lesbian mothers choose to share a household with another lesbian-mothered family in which the two mothers may or may not be in an emotional relationship. The mothers try to share child-care arrangements and expenses and to treat all the children in the household affectionately and without favoritism. There may be frequent family discussions to facilitate consistency in the relationships between the adults and the children.

Some lesbian mothers choose to live in an urban commune with other lesbians, or with lesbians and gay men and whatever children belong to the household. Their own children become integrated into the household and learn to relate to a variety of adults and children as "extended kin." Communal living situations can be the least expensive living arrangement for lesbian mothers, since the costs of rent and utilities are shared among several adults, and food can be bought in less-expensive bulk form. Again, in choosing to live in an urban commune, the mother is concerned that her principles are similar to those held by other members of the commune so that discrepancies are avoided in dealing with the children.

Mother's Partner and the Children

When a lesbian mother is in a relationship with another woman. they have to decide whether the partner will move in with the mother and her children. Some mothers prefer to maintain different residences; they may want to be able to focus complete attention on their children when they are with them, and to have time with their lovers without parental responsibilities. Sometimes they prefer to live apart to avoid exposure or to keep the knowledge of the relationship from the children. Or the relationship may be defined as a more temporary one, and the partners feel that they are not involved enough to live together. But, in general, when two women are deeply committed to each other, they usually want to live together as a family. This decision means a shift in the family constellation, and time and patience on the part of everyone concerned to adjust to the new situation. Many of the problems are the same as when the mother has a partner who is male, such as trying to balance the time and attention to the children while maintaining the new relationship.

The mother and her partner, though they live together, may decide that it is better to conceal the nature of their relationship from the children until the children are old enough to deal with its implications. Some women have lived together in the same house with the children for years, being always careful not to express undue affection for each other in the children's presence. However, with a stronger tendency toward being honest about one's feelings and clarifying ambivalences through discussion, fewer women feel the need to be so secretive.

Generally in a family in which the lover lives with the mother and her children, the partner has a job to help support the family, while the mother will spend more time caring for preschool

159

children if she can. Both share child-care responsibilities. In some arrangements, the mother and her partner may trade off working or going to school with child-care responsibilities for varying periods of time. Often the partner who lives in the home becomes integrated into the family circle and assumes broader responsibility for the children. She helps to make crucial decisions concerning the welfare of the family and contributes to the support of the household.

Often the partner develops an involved relationship with the children which both want to maintain even if the relationship with the mother breaks up. At Glide Memorial Church in 1972 one woman described her feelings about her lover's children:

> The children. I'm in love with the children. I have a different relationship with each one of them. As I've lived with them, I've taken more responsibility. I've changed roles in terms of them, made adjustments. . . . I'm not a "substitute mother," rather I'm a friend who loves them. It's the same as if adopting a child. It implies responsibility. . . . If anything should happen to their mother, and if either or both of them should wish to go with me, I'd consider very carefully what's best for them. If it was now, I'd take the kids until they had time to figure out what they want. I feel if at any point my partner and I couldn't have a healthy relationship, that wouldn't take me from my relationship with the children. I love them very much. I still want to be involved in the care of those kids and would try to live close by.

A woman who becomes the partner of a lesbian mother, especially if she has been used to the more socially oriented life of lesbians without children, may have difficulty in adjusting to the intense kind of domesticity entailed in living with a mother and her children. Sometimes, too, the children resent and refuse to accept the mother's lesbian partner. As with any serious relationship, it takes a strong commitment to the relationship and adjustment on both sides to make it work.

Breaking Up

Though many partnerships involving lesbian mothers last for years, sometimes they break up. It is always difficult in any breakup that involves children to explain to them why the family configuration in which they have been living is dissolving. It may be doubly difficult if the breakup with the children's father has taken place so recently that the children may be unduly affected by this new split, perhaps feeling, as children can, that they are in some ways responsible. Lesbian mothers who are concerned about their children are aware of this and try not to become committed or to expose their children to partners with whom there is little expectation of a long-term commitment.

Since lesbian relationships are not regulated by the courts, visiting rights have to be worked out informally. Many women try to remain friendly after breaking up, because of the relationship the partner has established with the children. Both women may feel that it would be too difficult for the children if the partners suddenly break off the relationship completely.

Some former partners, who are in new relationships, arrange to provide child-care or otherwise keep in touch with the children of the former partner, while drawing a new partner, if she is so inclined, into a relationship with the children as well. One couple baby-sits on a regular basis with the children of a former partner. The children enjoy this and like maintaining contact with a woman who once lived with them, while her new partner also takes pleasure in seeing the children.

Building a Substitute Kinship Network

As is often true with lesbians generally, lesbian mothers are often estranged from their families of origin. It is difficult for a single parent in an isolated situation to care for children, especially if there is worry about finances. Some of this strain is traditionally alleviated by grandparents or aunts and uncles of the children, who can baby-sit if they live in the area, or, if they live elsewhere, can supplement the children's needs with gifts. The lesbian mother is often denied these contacts and, beginning with her own small family, often has to create an alternative circle of friends and "extended kin" slowly and carefully. Often they start with other lesbian-mothered families, since they usually feel more comfortable in the company of other lesbian mothers socially. When in the company of the heterosexual mothers of their children's playmates, there is the added strain of maintaining an artificial social front. Even in the company of heterosexual friends who know about their lesbian feelings, there can be some guardedness. Therefore, for celebrations which are significant in our culture, such as national holidays, religious festivals, birthdays—times of an enhanced sense of isolation— lesbian mothers try to celebrate with other lesbian mothers and their children, substituting friendship networks for kin.

In addition to social and family events with the families of other lesbian mothers, the mothers try to establish a family type of relationship with a wide range of adults who have a continuous and affectionate relationship with the children. This helps to provide a range of models of adult behavior for the children, and assures them that there are many people who care about them. Children of lesbian mothers, then, can have a less rigid sense of appropriate adult behavior, since they are exposed to more kinds of people than are most children in nuclear family groups.

Many homosexuals have parental instincts, which they are able to act out to some extent by becoming involved with the family of a lesbian mother. Both lesbians and gay men often take the children on outings or offer to baby-sit with them. They enjoy the opportunity of being with the children, without the daily responsibility of raising them. Teachers, ministers, and other heterosexual friends of the family also serve as role models for the children, so that they have some exposure to heterosexual men, contrary to popular belief. As Carol Stack's study indicated (1970), children do not need a permanent male-role model to develop a sense of appropriate male behavior; rather, the children in her study were exposed to a series of men over several years and were able to form ideas of appropriate behavior without difficulty. Lesbian mothers, of course, try to see that their children are rarely exposed to sexist or bigoted adults of whatever sex or affectional preference.

A lesbian mother of three children ranging in age from ten to fifteen explained in a taped interview about developing such a group of adults to participate in family activities. She said that the children also took part in activities with other lesbian mothers and their children, so that they knew other children in their own social situation:

They also see other people aside from the gay women I associate with. We have other friends who are either sympathetic to gays—most of the people we come in contact with have a good idea that I'm a lesbian and some of these people are heterosexually oriented people—they are also homosexually oriented males, who take part in our family by taking the boys on trips or my daughter—both— camping, sightseeing, swimming, whatever it is. If they have time they do that. And then the heterosexual people they relate to are the people at church, the teachers at school, anybody that they see, they relate to in some way or other, so they know all of the options. Aside from heterosexuality, there are other things you can do and be.

Should the Children Be Gay or Straight?

There is an assumption among some heterosexuals that homosexuals who are exposed to children will, either by strong socialization or by some sort of "contagion," automatically turn the children into homosexuals. This assumption has had repercussions in the courts, when the homosexuality of the parent has been reason enough to break up a family, in the judgment of officials. It has wider repercussions in that known or assumed homosexuals have long been denied employment in jobs in which they had contact with children, such as social work, teaching, and recreation. Homosexuals point out that they themselves were raised by heterosexual parents in a culture in which homosexuality was stigmatized. Yet, in spite of early childhood training by heterosexuals, they are homosexuals. They also point out that homosexuality exists in most societies that we know about, in many historical contexts and among species other than human primates. (See Ford and Beach, 1951.) The assumption is that people will develop an affectional preference appropriate for them, whatever influences are brought to bear to the contrary.

Most lesbian mothers say that they do not care if their children are gay or straight, as long as they are happy with their choice and responsible to the people they love. They don't want their children to be expected to fit into a pattern of behavior that is alien to their nature, as they say children in most heterosexual families are raised. They stress that many of their own parents were rigid about sexuality, but that they themselves have the freedom to consider the personalities and needs of their own children, not the needs of the parents to socialize them one way or another. Examples are often given about how most middle-class parents try to stifle any indications in their children of characteristics thought to be the province of the opposite sex, to the ultimate cost to the child. Boys who were contemplative and sensitive were taunted as sissies and made to prove their masculinity. Girls who were more athletic and independent than was thought proper were a source of concern to their parents, who were certain that they would never be married, and could not imagine a viable alternative for them. One lesbian mother (in a symposium in 1972) described how she was allowing her adolescent son to develop more fully:

> I'm doing with my son what should have been done with his father. I'm liking him and loving him for who he is and allowing him, encouraging him, to cry if he feels like it ... to express his anger, disappointment, love. It's easier now for him to express his anger than his love. I want him to be a feeling human being who gets his identity from his ability to love, not his phallus.... It's important that both children [boy and girl] have the right to explore and express their feelings and get feedback about who they are. I want them to feel good about themselves from the strength of expressing their feelings.... We [in the family] let each other know our feelings; it's a sensitivity session. We try to stress tenderness and gentleness as better ways to relate to each other. We don't want the children's feelings to be cut off as ours were in our childhood. Our struggles may encourage kids to go on to other things besides worrying about their feelings.

During a discussion of lesbian mothers at a special Daughters of Bilitis meeting in 1973, most of the mothers present said that if their children were able to find a good love relationship, it didn't matter to them if their children were gay or straight. Yet, when pressed further, the mothers of boys said that they preferred that their sons not grow up to be gay. This attitude had partly to do with their stereotype of male gay life, in which, they believed, their sons would be influenced to have many partners and to relate to them superficially, rather than to develop any deep relationships. They thought the emphasis on sexuality, which they felt was typical of male homosexuals, was similar to the lack of commitment to emotional relationships that is thought to be characteristic of men in general compared with women.

Many of the mothers would not mind if their daughters grew up to be lesbians. They stressed, however, that it was entirely up to their children to decide which affectional preference was right for them. As parents, they would not try to influence them either way. Yet, their feelings that it would be more acceptable for their daughters than for their sons to be homosexual was influenced more by their own experiences than by alleged pressure on their children by homosexual parents. Many lesbian mothers have been disappointed in their relationships with men, yet have found significant emotional relationships with other women. In their experience, reinforced by feminist ideology, the qualities felt to be inherent in women—sensitivity, ability to show emotion, patience, and caring—suggest to them as mothers that a more satisfactory emotional relationship for their children of either sex is possible with women.

In practice, however, lesbian mothers usually support their children in whatever lifestyle the children feel is natural for them. As one mother put it, in a taped interview:

> The children must be people who can think for themselves and not be sheep, but have to be able to think and feel and know what they're doing is right for them, whether that includes sexuality or not.... The courts and prejudiced people don't realize that it's really fine to be gay. And if they're well-adjusted people, I see no reason why my children shouldn't be gay. But I don't see why they shouldn't be heterosexual, *if that's what they want to do.*

Though many lesbian mothers are striving to achieve a "liberated" kind of relationship with their children that would give adults and children alike an arena in which to fully develop their potential in the outside world, they face difficulties in maintaining this ideal. By adopting the lesbian-feminist lifestyle, by adhering to its principles in family relationships, and by developing a personal support group and an arena for public action within lesbian mothers' organizations, lesbian mothers have developed techniques that help to mitigate the influence of a larger culture whose values are antithetical to their own. In this way they play their part in the larger lesbian-feminist community by using their commitment to lesbian-feminism to structure their lives.

6.   WORLD VIEW

The history and development of the lesbian-feminist community in San Francisco has been described, including the contemporary aspects of community life. What has been documented are the changes both in personal and collective self-image and in the nature of social, political, and spiritual life. These shifts can be observed in the articulation of values by community members and how these affect personal interactions and the texture of community life.

In old gay times, as we have seen, lesbians felt isolated and vulnerable, largely because of their own acceptance of the stereotypes about homosexuals in the heterosexually dominated culture. As one of the informants said about bar life: "That's all I thought lesbians deserved." With the formation of the homophile organizations in the 1950s, the first step toward a more positive definition of self vis-à-vis the outside world was taken. Yet, the focus of these organizations, in keeping with the period, was on encouraging the outside world to accept the lesbian—that is, in Roxana Sweet's terms, on "norm-oriented behavior" (1968). The lesbian's sense of herself still depended in part on her acceptance by others on the terms of the larger culture.

The catalyst for radical change came with the liberation movements in the 1960s. The larger culture, by its very nature, was seen as having systematically oppressed various groups of people. Accordingly, its norms were no longer considered appropriate guides for blacks, for native Americans, for Chicanos,

166

for gays, and for lesbian-feminists who had been oppressed. Rather, the goal of the liberation movements was to change the system entirely, so that the old patterns of dominance and exploitation would be destroyed.

In the late 1960s, with the emergence of the women's movement, in which the concept of sexism was articulated as a social evil, lesbians realized that they too had been arbitrarily discriminated against, both as women and because of their affectional orientation. Lesbians who had lived lives of "woman-identification" and had to be more self-reliant than most women, found themselves in the vanguard of the women's movement. Some saw them as the purest form of liberated woman, since they were independent of men and reinforced their feminine strength in their daily lives by associating primarily with other women. Yet, so deeply ingrained was the fear of "contamination" by lesbians that even the most powerful women's organization, National Organization for Women, had what has been described as a lesbian purge[1] (Abbott and Love, 1972, pp. 118–134). This was one of the factors that led to the emergence of lesbian-feminism and, for some, separatism.

An important innovation, developed in the women's liberation movement, was also utilized by lesbian-feminists. This was small-group consciousness-raising, described as a "conversion process" in that one's entire personality and world view could become restructured in terms of the new ideology. (See Newton and Walton, 1971.) From this process came important innovations for lesbian-feminists: self-esteem and a sense of bonding with other lesbians; and the desire for action based on a new ideology—to use whatever skills and knowledge they had to build a self-sufficient community of lesbians whose behavior was based on a sense of sisterhood.

As we have seen, the development of that community was uneven, as the implications of old behavior patterns and lack of skills had to be contended with. Yet, techniques such as small-group sessions and criticism-self-criticism, coupled with a commitment to work out difficulties between community members, emerged to deal with discord.

1. The National Organization for Women later changed its direction to incorporate lesbians. Many chapters have Lesbian Task Forces.

From the field data and the perceptions of the women themselves, it appears that lesbian-feminist ideology has permeated many aspects of the lives of the women committed to it. Because of this commitment, personal relationships are expected to be egalitarian and supportive; child-raising methods incorporate these ideals and insure that they will be transmitted to descending generations as well as to new recruits to the community.

Women whose commitment to lesbian-feminism included an articulate political analysis acted on their politics by initiating and participating in a range of projects which addressed community needs. Some of these were designed primarily for lesbians, some included all women, while others took as their priority alliances between lesbians and other oppressed groups. But the result of all these enterprises, which ranged from sharing skills to education in health care, was to enlarge the pool of knowledge and skills available to the community as a whole.

Pragmatic gains within the community are not the only gains that have been made. The worlds of the spirit and of the mind have been enriched as well. Under the aegis of cultural matriarchy, there has developed a new sense of unearthing the "real" history of the contributions made by women and lesbians in the many areas in which they have been ignored. In the spiritual realm, new rituals and a reawakened sense of the nonlinear, intuitive aspects of life have been reaffirmed. This development has been felt by some to be necessary to counterbalance potential global destruction and to be the consequence of logical thought processes embedded in a competitive social system.

There has finally emerged a significantly different sense of self-worth and of the implications of the social role of the lesbian, not only on the part of the women involved but on the part of the larger society as well, albeit more slowly. This shift has had wider practical implications. Homosexuals, both female and male, have been recognized as a voting bloc in San Francisco. Because of this, legislation favorable to them has been enacted, and known homosexuals have been elected to office. Lesbian mothers have been reassessing their rights to their children and to a good life and have become politically active to achieve these goals. Rather than remaining closeted for fear of losing jobs, lesbians in professional fields have chosen to use their skills to further the cause of lesbian-feminism and to help their less fortunate sisters.

What has been documented are the social factors that influenced this shift, the character of lesbian-feminist ideology, and an assessment of the realities of its being acted on. We have examined a transitional phase in the larger picture of a redefinition of social roles and a reassessment of the implications of the society in which these roles were delineated.

This summary puts into sharp relief the underlying world view that emerged from the description of beliefs and observable behavior of community members. The concept of a world view, especially that of a literate, complex group such as the lesbian-feminist community, is a complicated one. Used in the present context, it can be defined as "the unspoken assumptions about the nature of ultimate reality" (Kluckhohn and Leighton, 1946, p. 303). Pragmatically, the world view of the lesbian-feminist community is a system of classification of people and relationships that makes a shared social reality possible.

It might be argued that in such a newly emerging community as that of the lesbian-feminists, an authentic underlying world view has not yet had time to develop. Yet, because of the nature of the experience of the women involved—most tellingly the transition from isolated old gay life to an identification with the lesbian-feminist community and its goals—certain consistent underlying assumptions can be discerned.

Not all of the following "unspoken assumptions" are shared by all women who identify themselves as community members, but they are implicit in attitudes and behavior as well as overtly stated in the interviews, to the degree that it can be concluded that they significantly affect the nature of community life. These, then, are some of the underlying assumptions about the nature of life, people, and relationships shared by members of the lesbian-feminist community.

The Self

The self is seen as life-affirming and composed of unfulfilled potential toward positive, complex development. It is hampered, however, by the arbitrary restrictions imposed by social roles and a limiting social structure. This is perceived as the result of centuries of male dominance, which has manifested itself most recently in the twin evils of capitalism and the nuclear family. But there is a component of the self which may be its saving grace—its inherent thrust toward growth. Therefore, it is believed, with the insights of feminism, the techniques of consciousness-raising, and the support of a community of like-minded women, the self can overcome the noxious effects of socialization in a male-dominated culture.

Classification of People

The world of humans is seen as divided into female and male. Within this division, females are divided into lesbian and non-lesbian. Another division, which includes all women (and sometimes extends to all oppressed people) but pertains most tellingly to the immediate lesbian community, is political/nonpolitical. Within the community itself, there is also the old and the new gay.

Men are seen, at best, as victims of their socialization. More usually they are defined as powerful, potentially violent, sexist representatives (and victims themselves) of the patriarchy, which has lasted for thousands of years and which has engendered a power-oriented, hierarchical structuring of the world, in which women, minorities, and the less powerful have been systematically oppressed.

Women are viewed as nurturing, intuitive survivors, who by their nature are more likely to be in harmony with the life force. If our present society had been structured in terms of women's characteristics rather than men's, some community members believe that all people would have had the opportunity to develop according to their potential, and cooperative, caring lives could be led by all. The political system of the realm of women might be called something like a "socialist matriarchy."

Children are seen as equal to adults, with less experience perhaps, but with their own contributions to make to the common good. Having their own integrity, they are not the property of their parents. The nuclear family is viewed as stifling the natural development of children, teaching them competitive attitudes, and inhibiting them by forcing them into rigid sex roles. Lesbian mothers have tried to use innovative child-raising methods to overcome what they define as the innate deficiencies of the heterosexually oriented nuclear family.

Lesbians are viewed as epitomizing the strength, the creativity, and the tenderness that is inherent in all women but is stifled in heterosexual women because they are trained to be dependent on and deferential to men. Lesbians are also seen as latter-day Amazons, fearless warriors, yet caring lovers and friends.

Nature of Relationships

There is a kind of contamination theory implicit in the structuring of lesbian-feminist relationships when it is felt that the more contact one has with men, the more one's inner strength and resourcefulness are sapped, since men, even inadvertently, try to dominate any situation and to cannibalize the strength of women.[2] Therefore, the lowest category of people is the sexist male. Next are heterosexual and bisexual women who associate with men. They are conceived as sometimes well intentioned, but not basically trustworthy because, it is believed, their real commitment is to men. Next are nonpolitical lesbians, with whom certain kinds of social activities are appropriate but with whom the deepest kind of bonding is not. Finally, politically oriented lesbian-feminists are seen as the most trustworthy and affirming, a vanguard of feminism in its purest form. The ideal is a community of lesbians with a core of politically oriented lesbian-feminists whose presence will serve to define and articulate the community. The community can influence other groups to nonsexist behavior and, in time, the boundaries of the community may be extended to include them as well.

Relationships between women, whether of friendship or of love, are between equals. They have two components: support, and the development of the potential of each person. Because of this concept, it is postulated that jealousy and possessiveness, anachronisms from the old culture, will become obsolete and that the community will be made up of mutually caring members.

Cosmology

The patriarchal godhead, symbolic of the heterosexual, male-dominated cultural milieu, has been interpreted as a source

2. Gerald Berreman points out that this concept is "the mirror image of Hindu beliefs about male/female relationships."

13. Lesbian and heterosexual women come together to chant at a Winter Solstice Celebration. (Laura Wilensky)

of repression of natural instincts and dominance by the powerful over the oppressed. As the entire world of linear thinking and hierarchies has been rejected, so has the godhead that exemplifies this view. The male godhead, finally, is seen as anti life.

Women are thought to be inherently deeply involved with the rhythms of the natural world. This involvement is personified by the concept of the Mother Goddess as a source of healing, intuitive thinking, and the unity of all sentient beings. The contemporary concept of the Mother Goddess is perhaps not historically "correct," but it has intuitive components of the resurgence of the female principle, the deep strength and caring of women. An awareness of whatever aspects of the concept of the Mother Goddess are appropriate to the individual woman provides a new source of resilience and insight about her "true" nature. This process can be intensified in a group context. Thus, group rituals have developed within the community which celebrate the Mother Goddess, while a resurgence of Wicca is part of this revived awareness of a strong female symbol.

The World

The heterosexual world is viewed by members of the community as "plastic," limited, and psychologically crippling.[3]

3. One community member talked about how she thought lesbians saw heterosexuals: "Gay people tend to stereotype heterosexuals as being very plas-

Perhaps an analogy might be made with the way in which Americans are viewed by some less affluent people—as clumsily attempting to be friendly and wanting to be liked, but in truth, potentially deadly, careless, and insensitive to the plight of those who have been annealed in the crucible of oppression and want. Many Americans have material advantages, but there is thought to be a concomitant widespread malaise of the spirit. In contrast, lesbians and other oppressed people, to the extent that they eschew material advantages and the rewards of the middle-class heterosexual world, have a nobility of spirit.

For the full development of each human to be possible, the political structures that hinder this must be overcome. From a community of women based on the principles of lesbian-feminist ideology and the emerging strength of its members, a new model for a righteous world will emerge. It is postulated that other groups of oppressed people will form communities based on their own characteristics and needs, and that the new world will be composed of loose coalitions of these self-contained communities. Part of the strength of a vision of a future is that it can be seen and celebrated in song and poem. Barbara Starrett's untitled poem about the nature of the new world, from an essay, "I Dream in Female: The Metaphors of Evolution" (in Covina and Galena, eds., *The Lesbian Reader*), embodies many of the concepts we have discussed. She writes: "I want to conclude with a fantasy, the beginnings of speculation about what art and life and women would be like in an evolved world based on

---

tic, just maintaining roles, not being real or able to really communicate. . . ." (The term "plastic" to describe American middle-class culture was first widely used by hippies in the middle 1960s to refer to an artificial lifestyle in which everything was locked into preconceived expectations that precluded real emotions or personal growth. (See Wolf, 1968.) She continues: "The idea is that straight women don't have an identity without their men, that they are weak and inept and incompetent. . . . I think lesbians definitely see men as very weak, frightened individuals who only know how to relate in terms of physical superiority. Straight society is the fat pompous male and the fat inept female. Fat, I think, has the symbolic effect of saying that they have more money than we do. We tend to think that we relate on a higher level, a more intense and deeper level, on a more pure communication level and that straight society is just functioning on a sexual level. (Note: this view is reminiscent of that of members of heterosexual society who feel that *homosexuals* relate only on a sexual level.) And men and women are manipulating each other for this purpose. . . . We think that we are further advanced as women and as people.

our own full emotional/extra-rational/spiritual/intellectual capacities":

> We are all holy
> We are each the mother and daughter of each
> We have no institutions
> No mediators between ourselves and our
> Experience our perceptions
> We are all singers
> We are all dancers
> We are all lovers and thinkers
> Painters and poets
> We are all teachers all learners
> The nourished and the nourishers
> We are all healers
> We are all builders and growers
> We have no experts no professions
> Whatever gives us the most pleasure
> That is what we choose to do and be
> We all benefit mutually
> From the intensities of each . . . .
>
> I am a gypsy a witch a seer
> My vision is only the beginning of visions
> A moment in the process of ourselves
> I know this:
> Whatever we will to be will be
> I know it is time to dream strong dreams
> And then to abandon them for the dreams to come.

14. *"We are all holy, we are each the mother and daughter of each." (Virginia Morgan)*

BIBLIOGRAPHY

Abbott, Sidney and Barbara Love
  1972.   Sappho Was a Right-On Woman: A Liberated View of Lesbianism. New York: Stein and Day.
Achilles, Nancy B.
  1964.   The Homosexual Bar. Ph.D. dissertation, Committee on Human Development, University of Chicago.
Adair Films
  1977.   Word is Out. San Francisco, Calif.
Aldrich, Ann
  1960.   Carol in a Thousand Cities. Greenwich, Conn.: Fawcett.
  1972.   Take a Lesbian to Lunch. New York: Macfadden.
Allen, Pamela
  1970.   Free Space: A Perspective on the Small Group in Women's Liberation. New York: Times Change Press.
Alther, Lisa
  1976.   Kinflicks. New York: Knopf.
Altman, Dennis
  1971.   Homosexual: Oppression and Liberation. New York: Avon.
Amazon Press
  1972–74.Amazon Quarterly. Oakland, Calif.
Anonymous
  1974.   Gay and Proud. Bay Guardian 9:2:12–27.
Anonymous
  1975.   Gay Moms, Gay Dads: A Special Report on Homosexual Parents. The Advocate, October 22, 1975:25–36.
Anonymous
  1976.   A Gay Time Is Had by 120,000 San Franciscans. Datebook, San Francisco Chronicle, November 1, 1976, p. 82.

Bibliography

Anonymous
   1971.   The Lesbian Experience. Cosmopolitan 170:2:174–178, 205.
Armanno, Benna F.
   1973.   The Lesbian Mother: Her Right to Child Custody. Golden Gate Law Review 4:1:1–18.
Armon, Virginia
   1960.   Some Personality Variables in Overt Female Homosexuality. Journal of Projective Techniques 24:292–309.
Atkinson, Ti-Grace
   1974.   Amazon Odyssey. New York: Links.
Bardwick, Judith M.
   1972.   Readings on the Psychology of Women. New York: Harper & Row.
Barnhart, Elizabeth
   1975.   Friends and Lovers in a Lesbian Counter-culture Community. In Old Family/New Family. Nona Glazer Malbin, ed. New York: Van Nostrand.
Basile, R. A.
   1974.   Lesbian Mothers. Women's Rights Law Reporter 2:2: 3–25.
Becker, Howard (ed.)
   1971.   Culture and Civility in San Francisco. Transaction, Inc.
   1963.   Outsiders: Studies in the Sociology of Deviance. New York: Free Press.
Bengis, Ingrid
   1972.   Combat in the Erogenous Zone. New York: Knopf.
Bloch, I.
   1933.   Anthropological Studies in the Strange Sexual Practices of All Races in All Ages. New York: Anthropological Press.
Boston Women's Health Collective
   1972.   Our Bodies, Ourselves. New York: Simon and Schuster.
Brown, Rita Mae
   1973.   Rubyfruit Jungle. Plainfield, Vermont: Daughters, Inc.
Bullough, Vern L.
   1976.   Sexual Variance in Society and History. New Yorker: Wiley.
Bunch, Charlotte
   1976.   Learning from Lesbian Separatism. MS 5:5:60–61, 99–102.
Bunch, Charlotte, and Nancy Myron (eds.)
   1974.   Class and Feminism. Baltimore: Diana Press (4400 Market St., Oakland, CA 94608).
Burton, Richard
   1956.   Terminal Essay to the Book of the Thousand and One

Nights. *In* Homosexuality: A Cross Cultural Approach. Donald Webster Cory, ed. Pp. 207–247. New York: Julien Press. (Originally published in 1886)

Caprio, Frank S.
1954. Female Homosexuality: A Psychodynamic Study of Lesbianism. New York: Citadel Press.

Cassell, Joan
1974. Political Lesbianism. Presented at the Annual Meeting of the American Anthropological Association.

Cavan, Sherri
1966. Liquor License. Chicago: Aldine.

Chafetz, Janet, Patricia Sampson, Paula Beck, and Joyce West
1974. A Study of Homosexual Women. Social Work 19:6:714–723.

Chesler, Phyllis
1972. Women and Madness. Garden City, New York: Doubleday.

Churchill, Wainwright
1967. Homosexual Behavior Among Males: A Cross-cultural and Cross-species Investigation. Englewood Cliffs, N.J.: Prentice-Hall.

Clark, Don
1977. Loving Someone Gay. Millbrae, Calif.: Celestial Arts.

Colette
1934. The Innocent Wife. New York: Farrar and Rinehart.
1966. Earthly Paradise. New York: Farrar, Straus and Giroux. (Originally published in 1936)
1967. The Pure and the Impure. New York: Farrar, Straus and Giroux. (Originally published in 1932)

Cordova, Jeanne
1974. Sexism: It's a Nasty Affair. Hollywood, Calif.: New Way Books.

Cory, Donald Webster
1956. Homosexuality: A Cross-cultural Approach. New York: Julien Press.
1965. Lesbianism in America. New York: MacFadden.

Covina, Gina, and Laurel Galena (eds.)
1975. The Lesbian Reader. Oakland, Calif.: Amazon Press.

Cronin, Denise M.
1974. Coming Out Among Lesbians. *In* Sexual Deviance and Sexual Deviants. Erich Goode and Richard R. Troiden, editors. Pp. 268–277. New York: Morrow.

Crosland, Margaret
1973. Colette: The Difficulty of Loving. New York: Bobbs-Merrill.

Bibliography

Damon, Gene, and Lee Stuart (eds.)
  1967. The Lesbian in Literature. San Francisco: The Daughters of Bilitis.

Damon, Gene, Jan Watson, and Robin Jordan
  1975. The Lesbian in Literature, second edition. Reno: The Ladder.

Daughters of Bilitis
  1956–72. The Ladder, San Francisco.

Davis, Elizabeth Gould
  1971. The First Sex. New York: Putnam.

Davis, Katherine Bement
  1929. Factors in the Sex Life of Twenty-two Hundred Women. New York: Harper.

de Beauvoir, Simone
  1953. The Second Sex. Translated by H. M. Parshley. New York: Knopf. (Originally published in 1949)

Devereaux, George
  1937. Institutionalized Homosexuality of the Mohave Indians. Human Biology 9:4:498–527.

Diner, Helen
  1965. Mothers and Amazons: The First Feminine History of Culture. New York: Julien Press. (Originally published circa 1929)

Douglas, Mary
  1966. Purity and Danger: An Analysis of Concepts of Pollution and Taboo. London: Routledge and Kegan Paul.
  1970. Natural Symbols: Explorations in Cosmology. London: Barrie and Rockliff.

Dundes, Alan
  1971. Folk Ideas as Units of Worldview. Journal of American Folklore 84:311:93–103.

Eisenstein, Zillah R.
  1973. Connections Between Class and Sex: Moving Toward a Theory of Liberation. Presented at the Annual Meeting of the American Political Science Association.

Ellis, Albert
  1951. The Influence of Heterosexual Culture on the Attitudes of Homosexuals. International Journal of Sexology 5:77–79.

Erikson, Erik H.
  1964. Insight and Responsibility: Lectures on the Ethical Implications of Psychoanalytic Insight. New York: Norton.
  1968. Identity, Youth and Crisis. New York: Norton.

Firestone, Shulamith
  1970. The Dialectic of Sex. New York: Morrow.

Fisher, Peter
  1972.   The Gay Mystique: The Myth and Reality of Male Homo-
          sexuality. New York: Stein and Day.
Ford, Clellan S., and Frank Beach
  1951.   Patterns of Sexual Behavior. New York: Harper & Row.
Forfreedom, Ann
          Sappho of Lesbos; Lesbian Tide. Part I, December 1973,
          Part II, January 1974.
Foster, Jeannette H.
  1956.   Sex Variant Women in Literature: A Historical and Quan-
          titative Survey. New York: Vantage Press, reprinted Bal-
          timore: Diana Press, 1975.
Frankfort, Ellen
  1972.   Vaginal Politics. New York: Quadrangle.
Freedman, Mark
  1971.   Homosexuality and Psychological Functioning. Belmont,
          Calif.: Brooks/Cole.
Freud, Sigmund
  1962.   Three Essays on the Theory of Sexuality. Translated by
          James Strachey. London: Hogarth Press. (Originally pub-
          lished in 1905)
Friedan, Betty
  1963.   The Feminine Mystique. New York: Norton.
  1976.   It Changed My Life: Writings on the Women's Movement.
          New York: Random House.
Gagnon, John, and William Simon
  1967a. The Sociological Perspective on Homosexuality. Dublin
          Review 512:96–114.
  1967b. Sexual Deviance. New York: Harper & Row.
Galana, Laurel
  1975.   Distinctions: The Circle Game. *In* The Lesbian Reader.
          Gina Covina and Laurel Galana, eds. Pp. 155–162. Oak-
          land, Calif.: Amazon Press.
Gay Academic Union
  1974.   The Universities and the Gay Experience: Proceedings of
          the Conference Sponsored by the Women and Men of the
          Gay Academic Union. New York: Gay Academic Union.
Gearhart, Sally, and William R. Johnson
  1974.   Loving Women/Loving Men: Gay Liberation and the
          Church. San Francisco: Glide Publications.
Giallombardo, Rose
  1966.   Society of Women: A Study of a Women's Prison. New
          York: Wiley.

Bibliography

Gibson, Gifford Guy
 1977. By Her Own Admission: A Lesbian Mother's Fight to Keep Her Son. Garden City, N.Y.: Doubleday.

Glazer-Malbin, Nona, and Helen Youngelson Waehrer (eds.)
 1972. Women in a Man-made World. New York: Rand McNally.

Goffman, Erving
 1959. The Presentation of Self in Everyday Life. Garden City, N.Y.: Doubleday.
 1963. Stigma: Notes on the Management of Spoiled Identity. Englewood Cliffs, N.J.: Prentice-Hall.

Goodland, Roger
 1931. A Bibliography of Sex Rites and Customs. London: George Routledge and Sons, Ltd.

Grahn, Judy
 n.d. Edward the Dyke and Other Poems. Oakland, Calif.: Women's Press Collective.
 1969. "Vera: From My Childhood," The Common Woman. Diana Press, 4400 Market St., Oakland, Calif. 94608.

Graves, Robert
 1955. The Greek Myths, Vols. I and II. London: Hazell Watson and Viney, Ltd.

Greer, Germaine
 1971. The Female Eunuch. New York: McGraw-Hill.

Grimstad, Kirsten, and Susan Rennie (eds.)
 1975. The New Women's Survival Sourcebook. New York: Knopf.

Gutter Dyke Collective
 1973. Dykes and Gorgons 1:1. Berkeley, Calif.

Hader, M.
 1966. Homosexuality as Part of Our Aging Process. Psychiatric Quarterly 40:515–524.

Haley, Mary Jean
 1971. What Gay Women Wear. Rags 10:20–21.

Hall, Radclyffe
 1928. The Well of Loneliness. New York: Covici Friede.

Harding, M. Esther
 1971. Women's Mysteries: Ancient and Modern. New York: Putnam.

Hays, H.R.
 1964. The Dangerous Sex: The Myth of Feminine Evil. New York: Putnam.

Hedblom, Jack H.
 1972. Social Sexual and Occupational Lives of Homosexual Women. Sexual Behavior 2:10:33–37.

182

Henriques, Fernando
1966.   Love in Action: The Sociology of Sex. New York: Dutton.
Henslin, James M. (ed.)
1971.   Studies in the Sociology of Sex. New York: Appleton-
Century-Crofts.
Heresies Collective
1977.   Lesbian Art and Artists. N.Y.: Heresies.
Hobson, Laura Z.
1975.   Consenting Adult. Garden City, N.Y.: Doubleday.
Hoffman, Martin
1968.   The Gay World: Male Homosexuality and the Social Crea-
tion of Evil. New York: Basic Books.
Hole, Judith, and Ellen Levine
1971.   Rebirth of Feminism. New York: Quadrangle.
Hooker, Evelyn
1957.   The Adjustment of the Male Overt Homosexual. Journal
of Projective Techniques 21:18–31. Reprinted in The Problems of Homosexuality in Modern Society. Hendrik M.
Ruitenback, ed. New York: Dutton. 1963.
1961.   The Homosexual Community. Proceedings of the XLV International Congress of Applied Psychology, Copenhagen.
1965.   Male Homosexuals and Their "Worlds." *In* Sexual Inversion: The Multiple Roots of Homosexuality. Judd Marmor, ed. Pp. 83–107. New York: Basic Books.
Hopkins, J. H.
1969.   The Lesbian Personality. British Journal of Psychiatry
115:1433–1436.
Howe, Irving
1976.   World of Our Fathers. New York: Harcourt Brace
Jovanovich.
Humphreys, Laud
1972.   Out of the Closets: The Sociology of Homosexual Liberation. Englewood Cliffs, N.J.: Prentice-Hall.
Iris Films
1977.   In the Best Interests of the Children.
Jacobus (Jacolliot, Louis)
1937.   Untrodden Fields of Anthropology. New York: Falstaff
Press. (Originally published circa 1898)
Jay, Karla, and Allen Young (eds.)
1972.   Out of the Closets: Voices of Gay Liberation. New York:
Douglas.
1975.   After You're Out. New York: Links.
Johnston, Jill
1972.   Return of the Amazon Mother. *MS* 1:3:90–93, 124.

1973.   Lesbian Nation: The Feminist Solution. New York: Simon and Schuster.

Karlen, Arno

1971.   Sexuality and Homosexuality. London: MacDonald.

Katz, Jonathan (ed.)

1971.   Homosexuality: Lesbians and Gay Men in Society, History and Literature. New York: Arno Press.

1976.   Gay American History: Lesbians and Gay Men in the U.S.A. New York: T. Y. Crowell.

Kearney, Michael

1975.   Worldview Theory and Study. Annual Review of Anthropology 4:247–270.

Kinsey, Alfred C., Wardell B. Pomeroy, and Clyde E. Martin

1948.   Sexual Behavior in the Human Male. Philadelphia and London: Saunders.

Kinsey, Alfred C., Wardell B. Pomeroy, Clyde E. Martin, and Paul H. Gebhard

1953,'70. Sexual Behavior in the Human Female. Saunders.

Klaich, Dolores

1974.   Women Plus Women: Attitudes Toward Lesbianism. New York: Simon and Schuster.

Klein, Carol

1973.   The Single Parent Experience. New York: Walker.

Kluckhohn, Clyde, and Dorothea Leighton

1946.   The Navaho. Cambridge, Mass.: Harvard University Press.

Koedt, Anne, Ellen Levine, and Anita Rapone (eds.)

1973.   Radical Feminism. New York: Quadrangle.

von Krafft-Ebing, Richard

1965.   Psychopathia Sexualis: A Medico-Forensic Study. Translated by Harry Wedeck. New York: Putnam. (Originally published in 1887)

Kuda, Marie J.

1974.   Women Loving Women. Chicago, Illinois: Womanpress.

Kushner, Tricia

1974.   Finding a Personal Style. *MS* 1:8.

Landes, Ruth

1940.   A Cult Matriarchate and Male Homosexuality. Journal of Abnormal and Social Psychology 35:386–397.

Lauradaughter, P. E.

Letter to the Editor. San Francisco Chronicle, October 28, 1976.

Lauristen, John, and David Thorstad

1974.   The Early Homosexual Rights Movement (1864–1935). New York: Times Change Press.

Lederer, Wolfgang
1968. The Fear of Women. New York: Grune and Stratton.
Leduc, Violette
1965. La Batarde. New York: Farrar, Straus and Giroux.
Lesbian Resource Center
1973. So's Your Old Lady. Minneapolis, Minn.
The Lesbian Tide Collective
1971-77. The Lesbian Tide. Los Angeles, Calif.
Leznoff, Maurice, and William Westley
1956. The Homosexual Community. Reprinted in The Problem of Homosexuality in Modern Society, Hendrik M. Ruitenbeck, ed. Pp. 162–174. New York: Dutton, 1963.
Louys, Pierre
1951. The Collected Works of Pierre Louys. New York: Avon. (Songs of Bilitis originally published in 1894)
McDermott, Sandra
1970. Studies in Female Sexuality. London: Odyssey Press.
Malinowski, Bronislaw
1927. Sex and Repression in Savage Society. London: K. Paul, Trench, Trubner and Company.
1929. The Sexual Life of Savages in Northwestern Melanesia. New York: Liveright.
Mantegazza, Paolo
1935. The Sexual Relations of Mankind. New York: Eugenics Publishing Company. (Originally published in 1885)
Marmor, Judd (ed.)
1965. Sexual Inversion: The Multiple Roots of Homosexuality. New York: Basic Books.
Marshall, Donald, and Robert C. Suggs
1971. Human Sexual Behavior: Variations in the Ethnographic Spectrum. New York: Basic Books.
Martin, Del
1970. If That's All There Is. Reprinted in Lesbians Speak Out. Pp. 72–73, 1974.
Martin, Del, and Phyllis Lyon
1972. Lesbian/Woman. San Francisco: Glide Publications.
Maslow, A. H.
1971. The Farther Reaches of Human Nature. New York: Viking.
Masters, William H., and Virginia E. Johnson
1966. Human Sexual Response. Boston: Little, Brown.
Mead, Margaret
1949. Male and Female: A Study of the Sexes in a Changing World. New York: Morrow.
1961. Cultural Determinants of Sexual Behavior. *In* Sex and

Internal Secretions, vol. 2, third edition, William C. Young, ed. Baltimore: Williams and Wilkins.

Miller, Isabel (pseud.)

1969.   Patience and Sarah. New York: McGraw-Hill. (Originally published as A Place For Us)

Millett, Kate

1964,'70. Sexual Politics. Garden City, N.Y.: Doubleday.

1974.   Flying. New York: Random House.

Morgan, Claire

1952.   The Price of Salt. New York: Coward-McCann.

Morgan, Robin (ed.)

1970.   Sisterhood is Powerful: An Anthology of Writings from the Women's Liberation Movement. New York: Random House, Vintage.

1972.   Monster. New York: Random House, Vintage.

Myron, Nancy, and Charlotte Bunch (eds.)

1975.   Lesbianism and the Women's Movement. Baltimore and Oakland, Calif.: Diana Press.

Nachman, Elana

1974.   Riverfinger Women. Plainfield, Vt.: Daughters, Inc.

Nathe, Patricia

1974.   The Hangout: An Ethnography of the Prickly Pear, a Bohemian Coffeehouse. Ph.D. dissertation, Department of Criminology, University of California, Berkeley.

Negrin, Su

1972.   Begin at Start: Some Thoughts on Personal Liberation and World Change. New York: Times Change Press.

Newton, Esther, and Shirley Walton

1971.   The Personal is Political: Consciousness-Raising and Personal Change in the Women's Liberation Movement. Presented at the Annual Meeting of the American Anthropological Association.

Nicholson, Nigel

1975.   Portrait of a Marriage. New York: Atheneum.

Nomadic Sisters

1976.   Loving Women. Sonora, Calif.: The Nomadic Sisters.

Onge, Jack

1971.   The Gay Liberation Movement. Chicago: Alliance Press.

Parker, Pat

1972.   Child of Myself. San Lorenzo, Calif. Shameless Hussy Press.

1973.   Pit Stop. Diana Press, 4400 Market St., Oakland, Calif. 94608.

1975. Quest: Women and Spirituality. Vol. 1, no. 4.

Radicalesbians

1970. The Woman-Identified Woman. Reprinted in Out of the Closets. Karla Jay and Allen Young, eds. Pp. 172–176. New York: Douglas (1972).

Richmond, Len, and Gary Noguera (eds.)

1973. The Gay Liberation Book. San Francisco: Ramparts.

Rodgers, Bruce

1972. The Queen's Vernacular: A Gay Lexicon. San Francisco: Straight Arrow Press.

Rosen, David H.

1974. Lesbianism: A Study of Female Homosexuality. Springfield, Ill.: Charles C. Thomas.

Ruitenbeck, Hendrik M. (ed.)

1963. The Problems of Homosexuality in Modern Society. New York: Dutton.

Rule, Jane

1975. Lesbian Images. New York: Doubleday.

Sagarin, Edward

1971. Sex Research and Sociology: Retrospective and Prospective. *In* Studies in the Sociology of Sex. James Henslin, ed. Pp. 377–408. New York: Appleton-Century-Crofts.

Salper, Roberta (ed.)

1972. Female Liberation: History and Current Politics. New York: Knopf.

San Francisco Women's Union

1975. International Working Women's Day. Pamphlet.

Sang, Barbara E.

1978. Lesbian Research: A critical evaluation. *In* Our Right to Love. Ginny Vida, ed., Pp. 80–87. Englewood Cliffs, N.J.: Prentice-Hall.

Sarachild, Kathie

1975. Consciousness Raising: A Radical Weapon. *In* Feminist Revolution. New York: Redstockings, Inc., Pp. 131–137.

Sharma, Umesh, and Wilfred Rudy

1970. Homosexuality: A Select Biography. Waterloo, Ontario: Waterloo Lutheran University.

Sherfy, Mary Jane

1972. The Nature and Evolution of Female Sexuality. New York: Random House. (Originally published in 1966)

Simon, William, and John H. Gagnon

1967a. Femininity in the Lesbian Community. Social Problems 15:212–221.

1967b. The Lesbians: A Preliminary Overview. *In* Sexual Deviance. John H. Gagnon and William Simon, eds. Pp. 247–282. New York: Harper & Row.

Sisley, Emily L. and Bertha Harris
1977. The Joy of Lesbian Sex. New York: Crown.

Sonenschein, David
1966. Homosexuality as a Subject of Anthropological Inquiry. Anthropological Quarterly 39:2:73–82.

Stack, Carol B.
1970. All Our Kin: Strategies for Survival in a Black Community. New York: Harper & Row.

Stearn, Jess
1964. The Grapevine: A Report on the Secret World of the Lesbian. Garden City, N.Y.: Doubleday.

Sweet, Roxanna Thayer
1968. Political and Social Action in Homophile Organizations. Ph.D. dissertation, Department of Criminology, University of California, Berkeley.

Task Force on Gay Liberation
1975. A Gay Bibliography: Fourth Revision. Philadelphia: American Library Association.

Tobin, Kay, and Randy Wicker
1972. The Gay Crusaders. New York: Paperback Library.

Tyler, Edward
1958. Primitive Culture. New York: Harper. (Originally published in 1871)

Vida, Ginny (ed.)
1978. Our Right to Love: A Lesbian Resource Book. Produced in cooperation with women of the National Gay Task Force. Englewood Cliffs, N.J.: Prentice-Hall.

Warren, Carol A. B.,
1974. Identity and Community in the Gay World. New York: Wiley.

Weinberg, Martin, and Alan P. Bell (eds.)
1972. Homosexuality: An Annotated Bibliography. New York: Harper & Row.

Westermarck, Edward
1906. The Origin and Development of Moral Ideas. New York: Macmillan.

Williams, Susan
1973. Lesbianism: A Socialist-Feminist Perspective. Seattle, Washington: Radical Women.

Wittig, Monique
   1971.   Les Guerilleres. Translated by David Le Vay. New York: Viking.
   1975.   The Lesbian Body. Translated by David Le Vay. New York: Morrow.
Whyte, William Foote
   1943.   Street Corner Society: The Social Structure of an Italian Slum. Chicago: University of Chicago Press.
Wolf, Leonard and Deborah
   1968.   Voices from the Love Generation. Boston: Little, Brown.
Wolff, Charlotte
   1971.   Love Between Women. New York: Harper & Row.
Women in Transition, Inc.
   1975.   Women in Transition: A Feminist Handbook on Separation and Divorce. New York: Scribner.
Women's Press Collective
   1974.   Lesbian Speak Out. Oakland, California: Women's Press Collective.
Wysor, Bettie
   1974.   The Lesbian Myth. New York: Random House.
Z Budapest and the Feminist Book of Lights and Shadows Collective
   1975.   The Feminist Book of Lights and Shadows. Venice, California: The Feminist Wicca.
Zaretsky, Eli
   n.d.   Capitalism, the Family, and Personal Life. Canadian Dimension.

INDEX

Index

Index

Designer: Louise Dunn

Composition: Lehmann Graphics

Lithography: Malloy Lithographing

Binder: Malloy Lithographing

Text: VIP Times Roman

Display: VIP Spartan Medium

Paper: 55 lb P&S Offset Smooth

Binding: Holliston Roxite B 51544